SECRETS OF A
METAPHYSICAL
FLIGHT ATTENDANT

REBECCA TRIPP WITH BRYNA RENÉ

BALBOA
PRESS

A DIVISION OF HAY HOUSE

Balboa Press books may be ordered through booksellers or by contacting:

Balboa Press
A Division of Hay House
1663 Liberty Drive
Bloomington, IN 47403
www.balboapress.com
1 (877) 407-4847

Because of the dynamic nature of the Internet, any web addresses or
links contained in this book may have changed since publication and
may no longer be valid. The views expressed in this work are solely those
of the author and do not necessarily reflect the views of the publisher,
and the publisher hereby disclaims any responsibility for them.

The author of this book does not dispense medical advice or prescribe the use
of any technique as a form of treatment for physical, emotional, or medical
problems without the advice of a physician, either directly or indirectly. The
intent of the author is only to offer information of a general nature to help
you in your quest for emotional and spiritual well-being. In the event you use
any of the information in this book for yourself, which is your constitutional
right, the author and the publisher assume no responsibility for your actions.

Any people depicted in stock imagery provided by Thinkstock are models,
and such images are being used for illustrative purposes only.
Certain stock imagery © Thinkstock.

Printed in the United States of America.

ISBN: 978-1-4525-8879-7 (sc)
ISBN: 978-1-4525-8880-3 (hc)
ISBN: 978-1-4525-8878-0 (e)

Library of Congress Control Number: 2013922775

Balboa Press rev. date: 01/02/2014

Contents

Introduction

"Wherever you go, there you are."

~ Jon Kabat-Zinn

My name is Rebecca Tripp, and this is the story of how I created my life.

In 1967, I embarked on the adventure of a lifetime. Flying at the forefront of the Women's Liberation movement, I left my hometown of Westport, Massachusetts to become a stewardess with United Airlines. During my thirty-five year career in the sky, the world changed. Local became global. "Stews" became flight attendants. Women became creative giants and corporate powerhouses.

And I became... me. While my physical form was flying from place to place, meeting new people and having life-altering experiences, I was simultaneously engaged in the long, often challenging journey within. At the tail end of it all, I emerged into the light of a new understanding of our world and how we as divinely human beings operate within it. I gained the power to be the best and most complete expression of myself in every moment.

This book is a chronicle of my adventures: the tale of a self-described glamour girl from Westport, Massachusetts who, after many setbacks, traumas, and triumphs, finally managed to find what so many people around the world are seeking: *a way to be truly happy.*

The stories in this book, which span from the 1960s to the present day, are my way to share with you the lessons I've learned. We are all capable of waking up—of stepping into the amazing powers and awareness we were born with. They say life is a journey, but the fun part is that we get to choose the destination. We even get to pick the color of the cushions on our beach chairs! All we have to do is decide what we really, truly want, and it will come to us. Our thoughts and feelings about our reality create our reality: what we believe is what we experience.

How do I know this? Because I've lived it. I've been a flight attendant, an entrepreneur, and a meditation teacher. I've lived a glamorous life as the owner of a New York modeling agency, and I've lived in hiding as a fugitive from an abusive spouse. I've been loved, and I've been raped. I've struggled with pain and disease—including cancer—and I've been spontaneously healed. I've been blocked by my own limiting beliefs, and I've been liberated from those same beliefs. I've been gloriously happy, and I've been haunted.

In short, I've lived a very human life among very human people. And yet, my life is far more than a jaunt through this three-dimensional realm. By connecting to the energy of the spiritual realm, I've learned to change my reality by changing my thought. My life exists now as I have created it.

Inner space is the new frontier, and the mind the new starship. Using the power of metaphysics and self-study, there is no problem that cannot be solved, no barrier that cannot be overcome. The only limits to what you discover are the limits you impose on yourself.

All things are possible. What we call impossible is, more often, simply unexplained. In this realm of the unknown lie the answers to our most burning questions. Why am I here? Is happiness real? How can I step out of suffering? How can I create the life I really desire?

Your answers to these questions will be unique, just as you are unique. The most important step toward finding them is to *open yourself to the possibility that the answers exist.* You *can* change your world, and the way you show up in it. Nothing is fixed. As our beliefs change, so do our experiences.

Through this story of my life, I offer you the tools to step into that openness. I can't tell you what you'll find there—no one can—but I *can* tell you that what you discover will be life-altering.

The Fourth Dimension

Most people I know, rich or poor, old or young, are unhappy. They're disgruntled employees in their own lives, convinced of their separateness from everything and everyone around them. Some suffer in financial lack, while others suffer in a house full of high-priced possessions. Some suffer in partnership; some suffer alone. Some suffer deeply, plunged into spirals of depression and addiction. Some suffer more quietly, going about their days and nights with discomfort buzzing in their ears like a fluorescent light bulb—something they can tune out for long stretches but which never really goes away.

The one thing we all have in common, it would appear, is our suffering. It's been called "the human condition," and it binds us across the lines of race, gender, economic status, education, and age. It's been analyzed, dissected, dramatized, vilified, idealized, and generally acknowledged to be the way of things since the dawn of mankind.

Over the ages, a cure for our collective condition has been offered by any number of religions and philosophies. Interestingly, when you sift through the dross of ceremony, doctrine, and dogma, all of these paths lead to the same place: union.

The cure for our separateness is *togetherness*—with our highest selves, with the absolute essence of the divine, and with one another. This integration is at the core of what

I teach, and is the unshakable foundation of my faith in myself and my ability to create my life as I desire.

In order to claim your birthright as a powerful, intuitive, abundant being using the tools in this book, you'll need to keep an open mind about spirituality. Why? Because we are, in essence, spiritual beings. Our energetic cores (our souls) are not made of mundane stuff. They're eternal, enduring, and connected to a Consciousness which exists beyond this three-dimensional plane. The keys to happiness and understanding lie in this other realm—a place I call the Fourth Dimension—and not in our impermanent human minds and bodies.

Why the Fourth Dimension, you ask? Didn't Albert Einstein propose that Time is the fourth dimension? Einstein did, in fact, make that statement. However, in the intervening years, it's been discovered by quantum physicists and spiritual masters that Time does not exist! It's a concept tied to the three-dimensional realm and the physical reality we perceive with our five senses. When it comes to the parts of us which are eternal (our higher selves, which are divine and divinely connected) Time has no meaning. Therefore, I choose to think of the spiritual dimension as the Fourth Dimension, only one step removed from our physical reality, and infinitely accessible.

In order to honor you, the reader, and your unique spiritual views, I've decided not to use the word "God" when talking about the fourth-dimensional Consciousness. That word can carry a lot of negative connotations, particularly those who have broken with the religious organizations of their childhoods. Therefore, I encourage you to let go of "God," and embrace "G.O.D."

Why G.O.D.? Because this acronym is simple, yet versatile. It means whatever you want it to mean! Take each letter and assign it a word of your choice. Some possibilities I like: Generous Omnipresent Divine, Grace Overpowers Doubt, and Great Open Door. These words have expansive energies that capture a spark of divinity, and no challenging associations.

In my experience, it doesn't really matter what you call the fourth-dimensional Consciousness: God, Yaweh, Allah, Buddha, Creator, Shiva, Shakti, Waheguru, Pan, Thor, Zeus, Ra, Ceredwin, Mother Mary, The Universe,

The Nameless... All is one, and one is all. When you follow the idea of G.O.D. far enough, all of these divisive names and identities can be realized as aspects of the same omniscient, omnipotent force. The name you choose to assign this force represents the aspect of the divine to which you relate most closely at this moment. But since there are literally millions of names for the Absolute, and to name them all would be the work of a lifetime, I'll just stick to our three simple letters—G.O.D.

Traveling... and Traveling

In this world, there are travelers, and there are Travelers.

The first are those who move their physical bodies from place to place: jet-setters, mobile businesspeople, post-grad adventurers. In my opinion, every trip is valuable. Travel is the strongest antidote for prejudice and bigotry that exists in our human world.

The second types, Travelers, are those who journey within as well as without. There's a shift happening in our world from materially-based thinking to spiritually-based thinking, and Travelers are at the forefront of this transition. Travelers roam the dynamic inner landscape in search of greater understanding, happiness, compassion, and inner peace, because they know that these things cannot be found in the material world. As they explore, they discover tools to deal with the unhelpful thoughts, patterns, and behaviors which block them from reaching their destination; these tools become their "survival kits," a collection of resources to be used and shared along the road of life.

A journey by air can very much parallel the journey through life, with all of life's attendant fears, frustrations, goals, and setbacks. Just as there are thousands of airplanes in the air at any given time, all headed to different destinations, so are there thousands of Travelers who have embarked on metaphysical journeys. Each of us starts in a different place, and ends up in a different place. Along the way, we have our own unique experiences—some joyful, some terrifying, some painful, but each an opportunity to learn and grow. And at the end, in one way or another, we all share the experience of *coming home.*

This book isn't a treasure map to your personal paradise; it's more like an atlas. I'll show you roads that might be fun to cruise for a while, but it's up to you to get out there and explore them. In other words, my purpose isn't to give you all the answers, but to show you how to discover your own answers. The anecdotes in this book are teaching stories. My experiences were unique, but the lessons contained within those experiences are universal. As you read, laugh, groan, or cry with me on my journey, I know that you will see reflections of yourself in the airplane window.

You'll also see reflections in this narrative of traveling and Traveling. Every experience we have is significant on two levels: the superficial or physical level, and the spiritual level. As you'll see when I talk about baggage, turbulence, and navigation, even things which seem mundane can mirror something deeper and more profound. As one of my spiritual teachers used to say, "You're not in the airplane, the airplane is in you."

There is a truth beyond what you've experienced; it's waiting for you. So sit back, relax, and enjoy the trip, Traveler. I know that wherever you end up will be fabulous!

CHAPTER ONE

Breakin' the Rules

"If I'd observed all the rules, I'd

never have gotten anywhere."

~ Marilyn Monroe

I n my thirty-plus years of flying the friendly skies, I found that you can tell a lot about people by the way they travel. People who love drama travel dramatically; people who are addicted to stress travel stressfully. The best travelers are those who can go with the flow and create a comfortable experience in what would otherwise be an uncomfortable place.

In the mid-1990s, a very good-looking man boarded my flight with his wife. As they took their seats, I watched in amazement. Out of their travel bags came two plush comforters, special pillows, a banquet of organic snacks, and fancy headsets. Piece by piece, the two of them proceeded to create an island of serenity amid the chaos of the first-class cabin. As they arranged themselves, I realized that I'd seen the man's face somewhere before: he was renowned author and filmmaker Michael Crichton, whose blockbusters included *Jurassic Park* and *The Lost World*.

After takeoff, it was clear that Mr. Crichton and his wife were totally relaxed in their private space. Rather than getting jittery about their flight or whatever awaited them at their destination, they acted as though they were on a picnic. Unlike many other celebrities I'd served, they made no arrogant demands. They barely noticed when someone jostled them in the aisle or when the plane jounced through a turbulent patch. When the man three rows in front of them started griping about the Chilean sea bass (I guess he was a chicken guy), it rolled right off them. Rather than expecting me, the pilot, their assistants, or their fellow passengers to provide them with what they needed to enjoy the flight, they *created their own experience.*

Maybe Mr. Crichton was able to do this easily because he traveled a lot. Maybe it was because, as an author of speculative fiction, he was used to living in his internal world and shutting out distractions. Maybe he'd just been a calm person all his life. Any way you look at it, the end result was the same: he enjoyed a much happier flight than the passengers around him. I was mesmerized. I'd never seen the concept of choosing an experience played out quite so explicitly.

The beauty of metaphysics is that it can teach us to do precisely that: *create our own experience.* With the right tools and a little practice, we can stay calm and centered even when life jounces us around.

The Big 'Why?'

I remember standing in the backyard with my mother on a beautiful summer day. I was young and "precocious" (as they called it in those days), and I had a hard time keeping quiet for long. As I watched my mother pin our laundry on the clothesline, a wave of questions flooded my mind. Where did we come from? How did we get here?

Why did women choose to wear skirts and men pants? Why did some people choose to smile while others frowned?

Aloud, I asked, because I badly wanted to know, "Why do people choose what they choose?"

In addition to my own boundless curiosity, I think my question was prompted by a sense of my mother's unhappiness. I wondered why she was sad when she could choose to be happy instead.

Looking back now, I understand her a bit better. When she was young, my mother was pretty and idealistic, a perky 1950s housewife. She was also a talented crafter and painter, and even spent time at art school. But whenever she dug out her easel, my father, a chemical engineer, would come home to see one of her paintings half-finished and proceed to criticize it. He wasn't by nature a cruel man, but in his world, everything about life was black and white, right and wrong. He thought he was being helpful, but his linear, logical mind couldn't encompass her artistic vision. Rather than argue about her process, my mother simply stopped painting. She suppressed her creative desires in order to maintain the outward appearance of a happy marriage.

When she got to be about forty, my mother... shifted. That's the only word for it. She could no longer keep her dreams alive. They were too painful, and the society in which she lived wasn't likely to accept any change in her circumstances (e.g., divorce). Once she shut down her dreams—of a nurturing relationship, of art and creativity, of freedom—she became a different person, as pragmatic as she had once been idealistic. Her choices might have shielded her from my father's criticism, but they didn't make her happy.

When I asked my question in the yard that day, my mother was still young—not yet thirty—but "reality" was already starting to set in. She looked down at me, confused, and said, "I don't know why people choose things. They just do."

I wasn't satisfied with that answer. So I kept asking my question.

I entered first grade with high expectations. I wanted to learn to read so badly. Every time someone picked up a book or a newspaper and read aloud the words that were printed there, I thought it was the most amazing thing— like magic, or a secret code.

On my first day of school, I was terribly excited. I felt like a spy in a foreign land on a mission to decipher this cypher which unlocked so many doors.

The teacher instructed the class to sit in a circle around her. Everyone was very nervous. I'd learned to whistle the day before, and it seemed like a cheerful thing to do, so I pursed my lips and started making music.

The teacher shook her finger at me and said firmly, "Rebecca! We do not whistle in school."

"Why not?" I was totally confused. I thought being able to whistle was a good thing.

"Because it's against the rules," she replied.

A few of my classmates snickered. Disoriented and a little embarrassed, I stopped whistling. I'd been looking forward to this day so intensely—and yet here I was, knocked flat in the first few moments. What kind of place was this school that didn't allow whistling? And who made "The Rules," anyway?

I received part of my answer in my twenties. Studying the writings of philosopher George Ivanovich Gurdjieff, I was fascinated by his assessment of morality. According to his theory, we're programmed by our parents, culture, background, and religion to adhere to "The Rules," whatever those may be. When we question those rules, we're answered with a shake of the head and a flat, "Because that's the way things are."

Funny that "the way things are" can be different for every person in every part of the world. What is perfectly acceptable in one culture may be a mortal sin elsewhere. When we step outside what we "know" and look at the bigger picture, we begin to see that none of these rules are divine or immutable. They only exist because we've established them for ourselves.

Through my years of study, I've learned that divine principles are those of love, unity, and compassion— principles that draw all living creatures together into a seamless, integrated whole. But in almost every case, rules divide us. They create fear, distrust, anxiety, guilt, and anger. The Rules told my mother that she should choose the role of "the good wife" over her passions and dreams, and that how she felt was less important than how society perceived her.

Women's Liberation, the movement we now know as feminism, changed the role of women in society forever, but when my mother was making her choices, this movement had yet to take root. Even today, after decades of change, there are still traces of those old rules to contend with. Women aren't expected to be housewives. Nor are men expected to be breadwinners. However, for many, the need to maintain a façade of success, competence, wealth, and "good" relationships, even at the expense of our happiness, is just as strong as it was sixty years ago.

No matter how old we get or how much we think we know, our internal programming governs nearly every aspect of our lives—right up until the moment when we wake up and realize *we can make our own decisions*. The rules don't have to dictate the parameters of our reality. We can all pull a Michael Crichton and create our own experience.

My first-grade teacher wasn't a bad woman, but her programming controlled her. For whatever reason, she didn't feel it was right to allow a child to make joyful noise. Maybe she was unhappy, and my happiness irritated her. Maybe she was afraid of what the school principal would say if she allowed me to break The Rules. Maybe she was afraid I'd start a full-fledged first-grade rebellion. Who knows? But her words stuck with me, and I'm grateful. They helped spur me toward many fascinating discoveries I might never have made otherwise and a career that took me to every corner of the globe.

Still, if I could travel back in time and become my six-year-old self again, I would keep whistling. Because that rule was bogus.

Flight Path

In the days before security lines, body screening, sardine-can seating, and puny five-dollar bags of almonds, there was a romance to flying. There were real glasses from which to sip wine and brandy. There were five-star meals in first class. Flying was seen as something that only adventurous, wealthy, sophisticated people did. But gradually, the world changed, and the airlines changed along with it. Once the airborne equivalent of the Love Boat, an airplane is now barely more than a subway car in the sky.

In many respects, the high idealism of the middle twentieth century is going the way of the airlines' golden age. A lot of people are beginning to realize that there's more to life than what we've been shown. The material wealth and security of the American Dream is an empty shell. Happiness can't be purchased with hard work. The clothes don't make the man (or the woman), nor does the house, the car, or the iPhone. Instant gratification doesn't equal lasting contentment.

In other words, The Rules aren't serving us anymore. Maybe they never did.

When we realize this, not only intellectually but wholly, we take the first steps toward a new way of being. When we wake up, we begin to see that there is more to life than what our five senses tell us—more than what can be counted or controlled in the form of material things. Just as if we were flying, we rise above the daily dos and don'ts and the limiting structure of The Rules to gain a clearer perspective. We learn that who we are doesn't depend on the house we live in, the clothes we wear, the person we sleep with, or even the way our friends view us. Rather, we discover that we are all part of a single, universal whole.

These are hard truths to assimilate. They go against The Rules. How can a struggling high school janitor be "worth" as much as a guy with a degree from Yale and a seven-figure salary? How can a penniless refugee be "worth" as much as a movie star? But it's true. Underneath the colorful trappings, the shield of ego, and The Rules, we are all made up of the same carbon, water, and electrical impulses. We all want the same basic things: to feel loved, connected, valued, and supported.

From the air, it's impossible to tell if someone is black or white, rich or poor, smart or stupid, jaded or innocent. The only thing you can say with any certainty is, "That's a person." In the Fourth Dimension, where divine principles govern, there is no such thing as "survival of the fittest." There is only unity. If you climb high enough, the lines between cities, counties, states, and nations disappear. Go higher still, and you can see for yourself that all rivers really do lead to the sea, and that all seas flow into one another. Everything is part of everything else.

If you take yourself outside the daily world of family, spouses, church, friends, and rivals, you might experience something similar. You might begin to see the invisible shackles of The Rules that shape your thoughts and behavioral patterns, and how they influence your choices. If you fly high enough, or step far enough outside your norm, you might come to a place where you can leave The Rules behind, and let the divine principles of love, unity, and abundance take precedence.

Not a single one of these lofty ideas was present in my consciousness when I first became a stewardess.

When I was twelve, my father came home from a business trip with a blank job application for Eastern Airlines. With a smile, he handed it to me.

"You think I should be a stewardess?" I asked.

"It might be a good thing for you someday."

I was immediately intrigued. As my father had already figured out by the time he brought me that application, I wasn't cut out to be a housewife. I was too headstrong, too adventurous; I wasn't interested in what a traditional life could offer. More, the dream of flying had been with me all throughout my childhood, and I understood, on a subliminal level, that flight meant freedom—a way out of an ordinary, ho-hum life on the ground. I loved the way that, from the air, all the things I thought were so big suddenly became small. From above, the world looked perfectly ordered, like it was all laid out according to some master plan.

Over the next couple of years, becoming a stewardess occupied more and more of my thought. Once, I went with my mother to T.F. Green Airport in Rhode Island to pick up a relative. I had to pee, so I made my way through the crowded baggage claim area toward the ladies' room. Lo and behold, two stewardesses stood before the mirrors, touching up their already-perfect makeup. In their navy-blue uniforms, jaunty hats, scarves, and heels, they looked like goddesses of the sky. I was enthralled all over again. Someday, I promised myself, that would be me. Someday, little girls would gape at me as I applied my lipstick in Miami, or Casablanca, or Paris.

I held on to the dream of flying through high school. I did well in all my classes, but there were some big questions about what I would do after graduation. I couldn't become a stewardess until I turned twenty, and there was no way I was going to work at the Westport Five-and-Dime for two whole years. My mother, frustrated, asked my school guidance counselor for advice. The answer: "She's a pretty girl. She'll get married and you won't have to worry about it anymore."

In the end, I tagged along with my high school boyfriend to Westfield State College, where I enrolled in the teaching program. I had no intention of finishing the four-year program, but taking core classes in trigonometry and world history was far more interesting to me than what my girlfriends were doing back home, which mostly involved hunting for eligible bachelors.

Halfway through our freshman year, my boyfriend asked me to marry him.

I looked at him askance. "What do you think I would do if we got married?" I asked.

"You could work in the Five-and-Dime until I get out of college," was his answer. "Then, you'll be pregnant, so you won't have to work anymore." The way he delivered this assessment, it sounded like a sales pitch. "We'll buy a house near the water, and we'll—"

"Don't you know me better than that?"

Obviously not. When we broke up a week later, all I could feel was an overwhelming sense of relief.

Fast-forward fourteen months. It was 1966, and I was in my second year at Westfield State. I had a new boyfriend and a new sense of independence after living on campus for nearly two years.

One weekend, I came home to my parents' house to visit, do some laundry, and relax a bit. On Saturday night, the boy I was dating picked me up in his parents' car and drove me up to New Bedford. We parked in our favorite spot, an overlook from which we could see the lights of Martha's Vineyard shimmering across the bay. We weren't alone—this was a popular spot for couples—but it was dark, and we felt comfortably anonymous as we cracked a couple of beers and snuggled up together on the wide bench seat.

As I gazed dreamily out over the water, I suddenly saw three lights hovering on the horizon. They came closer and closer, skimming over the water. They were saucer-shaped, about as big as an automobile, and blinked on and off with a red-orange light. They soared and bobbed and performed a few amazing right-angle turns, but always returned to their V-shaped formation.

The UFOs (because I knew even then that's what they were) drew nearer until they were hovering almost directly overhead. I could see them clearly, even in the darkness—and I wasn't the only one. People around us got out of their cars, whispering in fearful disbelief. The whole experience was strange, otherworldly.

After a minute or so, the saucers turned and, without warning, whipped back out to sea. We watched, stunned, until they disappeared. I wondered briefly if the saucers were government-built, but discovered that I didn't really care. Whether the Air Force or Martians had constructed them, the very fact that such engineering was possible blew my thought wide open.

My boyfriend and I were, of course, very excited. We talked about the saucers the whole way home. Not long after he dropped me off, he called to say that he had contacted Otis Air Force Base on Cape Cod to report what we'd seen. According to him, the Air Force didn't know anything about the saucers, and there had been no aircraft in the area. But my boyfriend's report was not the only one filed that night.

On May 13 of that year, I finally turned twenty. As soon as my spring classes ended, I retrieved that old application for Eastern Airlines from the treasure box on my bureau. Giddy with excitement, I filled out the somewhat dog-eared application, and sent it in. I also picked up applications for United Airlines, American Airlines, and TWA.

A few weeks later, I received a request for an interview with Eastern's management team in Boston. Soon after that, I received another letter, this one containing a round-trip ticket to Miami and a voucher for an all-expenses-paid hotel room. I was literally on cloud nine. My childhood dream was coming true!

The interview in Miami was a bit more intensive than the chat I'd had in Boston. The Miami boss asked me to put on the Eastern Airlines hat, and walk around the room so he could check out my posture. Then, he moved me to the window, where the light was strongest, and proceeded to examine my pores. He even peered inside my mouth to look at my teeth. I'd known that looks were important in the airline business, but this was a little over the top! When he hired me on the spot, it was a nice boost to my ego—but a small voice in my heart urged me to think about it for a few days.

Back in Boston, I was called in for another interview, this time with United Airlines. They also offered me a job, and after a bit of back-and-forth, I decided to accept. United was a bigger airline than Eastern, and they seemed genuinely interested in what I had to offer their company (beyond my great teeth, of course).

The UFO sighting definitely added a sense of urgency to my career path. I wondered what else might be up there in the sky, just waiting to be discovered. The Rules were different up there, I knew. What's more, the sighting had redirected me back to the question I'd been asking since I was a little girl, the question which I now know characterizes seekers of all faiths and disciplines.

Why?

What are Your Rules?

When I took off to become a stewardess, I broke all kinds of rules. My parents weren't shocked, but they weren't pleased, either. They came from a generation where women got married and had babies, period. They'd been leery enough of my choice to go to college. I think my mother may also have been a bit resentful of the freedom I'd chosen. She lived in a world where housewives numbed their pain with little blue pills, and where suicide was considered preferable to divorce. She got all kinds of flak from her friends about her wayward, headstrong daughter.

What is interesting to me to recall is that although I was rebellious, I wasn't fearless. I actually had a great deal of fear around what were, in the mid-1960s, my very unusual choices. Would saying no to marriage while I was still young and beautiful mean ending my life as a lonely spinster? Could I continue to fit into the culture of my hometown if I didn't want to be someone's wife? But as much as I feared the repercussions of breaking The Rules, I feared living as their prisoner much more.

When you live totally in the three-dimensional realm, you can find yourself imprisoned by The Rules. Everywhere you turn, there's another "should" or "have to" to deal with. There are rules about sin, disease, death, wealth, and health. There are rules about socialization, testing, competition, "survival of the fittest," earning, learning, and giving. Boxed in by so many rights and wrongs, it's easy to think what's out there is running your life—when in reality, your own belief in The Rules is the only thing holding you in thrall.

Gurdjieff wrote that we are asleep until we wake up through "self-remembering." When we awaken to the truth that only the divine principles of love, health, abundance, unity, and reciprocity can give us the security we're looking for, we can start to play by the rules *we* choose, not the ones handed down to us. But until we make the leap into understanding that The Rules are not real, we will not find peace.

It's no secret that our culture does not promote asking the big questions. We are predominantly left-brained and programmed to remain that way. Once you no longer have

The Rules to tell you what to do, you become responsible for your own life. Everything happens because you choose to allow it. You have to get creative, and you have to be willing to change. Your current situation is no longer the fault of society, religion, your parents, or your friends. Once you realize that you make your own rules, the consequences are yours to own.

It is also interesting to observe that some people *need* rules. They're completely comfortable with the way in which their lives have been mapped out for them, and want to do everything just the way they're told. They need the guidance of religion or society to tell them what is right, and what is wrong. Their adherence to routine is practically an addiction. They might experience some occasional, vague sense of unhappiness, but it's not enough to spur them to action.

If you're reading this book, I think it's safe to assume that you are not one of those people. Therefore, it's your task to identify The Rules as they exist in your life, and decide which of them need breaking.

The Square Block Phenomenon

When you start playing by your own rules, you move from the realm of the physical into the realm of the metaphysical.

Metaphysics is a branch of philosophy concerned with discovering, and in some small way explaining, the fundamental nature of being. The word "metaphysical" is Greek in origin, from *metá*, meaning "beyond," and *physika*, meaning "physical" or "of matter." Thus, metaphysical people attempt, through various means, to better understand the world that lies beyond the reach of our five senses. I like to call it the science of internal exploration.

Students of metaphysics understand that there are things beyond our current understanding. They question established beliefs and popular programming (aka, The Rules), and instead seek the truths at the core of things— those divine principles I referred to earlier. Disciplines as varied as Yoga, Christian Science, Buddhism, Silva UltraMind, Reiki, Transcendental Meditation, Druidic mysticism, Wicca, and Kabbalah can all fall under the heading of "metaphysics," if they are used as vehicles through which to understand the divine principles and our relationship to G.O.D., the divine Consciousness of the Fourth Dimension.

If followed far enough, any spiritual path will lead you to the same conclusion: *what we perceive as real is governed by our thought, and our thought is governed by anything we accept as unchangeable.* All progress, spiritual or otherwise, begins with someone's refusal to adhere to the accepted definition of "possible."

Several years after I started flying, I ran into the boyfriend who was with me during the UFO incident. Although he had been the one to call Otis Air Force Base that night, and had been at my side throughout the entire experience, he didn't remember a thing about our sighting. His brain, afraid of what accepting this mind-blowing experience might mean to The Rules he lived by, had erased the memory entirely.

The mind, untrained, can be a self-defeating creature. It has a way of circumventing evidence to maintain its own preconceptions, especially when it comes to its favorite

Rules. In order to fully experience a metaphysical journey, you need to be able to accept what your heart, soul, and intuition show you, even if no one else can see what you see. You also need to learn the difference between your mind's habitual fabrications and the real deal. It's a fine line, and one that takes time to learn to navigate.

A closed mind is like a wooden door with a square hole in it. The viewer—the owner of the mind—sits behind that door. All the closed mind sees are the pieces of evidence which are able to slip through that square hole: square blocks. Do round blocks exist? Of course! So do triangular blocks and octagonal blocks. But while the door remains closed, square blocks are all the viewer will ever get, and all he can ever expect to see. That's how my old boyfriend could forget so completely about our UFO sighting: it wasn't a square block. Rather than alter his mental paradigm by opening the door, his mind simply refused to allow the evidence to be admitted.

Our mental filters are far more subtle than square holes, of course, but they're just as divisive. They tell us that we feel certain ways about people, places, and events, and then instruct us to apply those feelings to people, places, and events that haven't yet entered our experience. They tell us what is and isn't possible, and what is or isn't likely. The more Rules we have, the more filters are applied. Soon, we're carrying around a house full of doors, closing off whole categories of experience.

I have no doubt that I saw those UFOs. I have evidence that other people saw them, too. I have also had experiences which no one else has shared—and I don't doubt those either, because they were real enough to point me in the direction I needed to go in order to continue to grow, learn, and expand my consciousness. They showed me where The Rules fell short, and where G.O.D. was present and waiting on the other side of the door.

CHAPTER TWO

See It, Believe It
(Imagination Equals Creation)

"Everything you can imagine is real."

~ *Pablo Picasso*

After I was hired by United, I packed my suitcases, said goodbye to my sleepy New England hometown, and set out for stewardess school in Des Plaines, Illinois.

Back in those days, stewardesses weren't merely drink-serving referees: we were the bait to entice people to fly. We were expected to project an image of upper-class hostess, doting wife, and seductress all rolled into one. We had to have killer looks and a whole slew of skills. We learned to serve meals with the grace and skill of waiters in five-star restaurants, soothe unruly children with games and twinkly smiles, and light men's cigarettes with all the sultry sauciness of a brigade of Marilyn Monroes. We were welcoming, charming, and sexy as hell—and we loved every minute of it.

Looking back, I can see that we were objectified, but I never felt victimized by the nature of my job. My power wasn't the same as the power flaunted by our first-class male fliers, but I *did* have power—over my own life, my own money, and my own choices. I wasn't being pressured to get married and have babies, like so many girls in my hometown; in fact, if I'd chosen those things, I would have lost my job, because at that time stewardesses were required to be single and unattached. Back in the 1960s, when Women's Lib was still in its infancy, perpetual singleness seemed like a pretty sweet deal. If I had to act like a high-class housewife, at least it was only for five or six hours at a time; after that, I could do whatever I pleased, with whomever I pleased. I didn't have to settle for a life that didn't feel authentic to me.

After completing school, I moved into what was affectionately called a "Stew Zoo" on Belmont Avenue in

Chicago's North Shore neighborhood. While the airline didn't own apartment buildings for its employees, it did recommend safe, affordable housing. Because we were always coming and going at odd hours, we appreciated the extra security, and flocked to these properties like so many turtle doves.

My building was managed by a short, chubby, bald man named Dickie, who lived in an apartment by himself on the top level of the building. He was the go-to guy for everything: backed-up toilets, noisy neighbors, and the occasional late-night escort to and from the train station. He was building super, security guard, and confidante all in one. Sometimes I pictured him as a rotund little sultan, surrounded by his harem of beautiful sky goddesses.

Stews weren't the building's only residents; we just made up the majority. There were a couple of families, a few old-timers, and a number of single men whose highest priority in real estate was to be surrounded by a bunch of gorgeous, unattached women.

Ron was one of these men. He was thirty-five, with wavy brown hair and intense eyes, a sort of young Sinatra. He and his roommate Dave were business partners in a multi-level marketing company, and had money coming out their ears. They wore silk suits and alligator shoes, and drove brand new matching Cadillac El Dorados, which they'd paid for in cash. They took me and my roommate Sara out often, and introduced us to the elegant side of Chicago.

While we never officially dated, Ron and I became good friends. He taught me one of the single most important lessons of my life.

One night, Ron, Sara, and I were hanging out in my apartment, drinking White Russians and cracking jokes. As the night wore on, the conversation turned more serious. I started telling Ron how I yearned to live in New York City. Chicago was nice and all, but New York was the bastion of glamour, and seemed like the perfect home base for a twenty-year-old Stew with an adventurous spirit. Problem was, I didn't see how I could make it work. I hadn't been flying long enough to feel right about asking for a transfer. Also, I wasn't often in New York for more than a twenty-four hour layover, so how could I find the right place to live? Even my naïve, idealistic little self knew that there were neighborhoods in New York where you didn't want to be traipsing about by yourself at 3 a.m.

"Well, sweetheart," Ron drawled in his best Rat Pack voice. "You've come to the right man."

"What? You have a place in New York?" It wasn't out of the realm of possibility. Ron took great pleasure in astounding me with tales of his latest acquisitions.

"No, no. This is better than that. I'm going to teach you something my uncle taught me years ago. You can use the power of your mind to create exactly what you want. All you have to do is imagine yourself in your perfect apartment, in the perfect neighborhood, for the perfect price."

He went on to tell me that this technique was called *creative visualization*, a powerful tool that harnesses the creative brain to create a new, improved physical reality. This technique has since been publicized in books like *The Secret*, and is taught by coaches and gurus around the country. In fact, the principles Ron shared with me that night are very similar to the visualization exercises created by José Silva, the well-known parapsychologist whose Silva

UltraMind techniques I studied (and eventually taught) in the 1990s.

Back in 1968, however, creative visualization was still, well, a secret. To the general public, anything to do with thought energy, manifesting, or alternate realities was the province of hippies and weirdoes.

Of course, I fell in love with the concept immediately. I'd already seen a UFO. I knew there were things in this world beyond my understanding. This was just the next reality challenge to come my way.

"I'm listening," I said.

"Here's what you do. Think of three things you want to attract into your world. Write them down on a piece of paper in the present tense, as if you already have them."

"So, I should write, 'I have a gorgeous apartment in Manhattan?'"

"Exactly. Take that piece of paper and put it next to your bed. Before you go to sleep, and when you wake up in the morning, hold that paper and feel the way you'll feel when you have what you want. You can even talk about it out loud to yourself."

At this point, Sara stuck her fingers in her ears. "You two are insane!"

I guess we were wandering outside The Rules as she knew them. I ignored her. "So what's on your list right now?" I asked Ron.

"I can't tell you. That's one of the keys to making this work. When you tell other people that you have something, or you've done something, it's like completing your action, so the manifestation is confused. Plus, you don't want to dilute your feelings with other people's doubts." He waggled his eyebrows at Sara, who pulled a face at him. "But my uncle said that when you really believe something is true, it has no choice but to show up in your life."

"Like a self-fulfilling prophesy," I breathed. "That's so *cool!*"

Ron lifted his glass in a toast. "Cheers, darling!"

Buzzing with power and possibility, I started my creative visualization practice that very night. I saw myself getting the transfer I wanted without any hassles or delays, and moving into my beautiful, convenient, affordable apartment in New York City. I saw myself creating an exciting life in the sky among dynamic, interesting people. As I fell asleep, I could almost hear yellow cabs honking their horns outside my window.

I never doubted that Ron's technique would work, but the ease with which everything showed up astounded me. Two months later, my transfer was complete: no questions asked, no bureaucratic delays. I found an apartment in a gorgeous building with a doorman and lots of security features, right on the corner of 37th and Lexington. It had gigantic windows, spotless wood floors, and a balcony—all within my budget. The landlord even partially furnished the apartment at no extra cost! Plus, Sara (who'd come around a bit since that first conversation with Ron) agreed to move with me, which saved me the trouble of finding another roommate.

(In case you were counting, the third thing on my manifestation list was a fur coat. It was delivered to me with the same ease with which the apartment and the transfer materialized. I know what you're thinking: "A fur coat? Really?" Yes, I was a bit shallow in those days. But I strutted that coat all around New York, Paris, and Milan, and it felt great.)

I was so excited about this new way of thinking that I shared it with anyone who would listen. Most people reacted as Sara had, with a lot of "Oh, really," and "You're crazy!" But others, especially those my own age, were receptive. It was 1968, and people like Timothy Leary were starting to introduce new thought paradigms, issuing quotes like, "If you don't like where you are, you can always pick up your needle and move to another groove." In a sense, that was exactly what I had done with my manifestation. I had taken the old record off of the player, and shifted to a different soundtrack.

A few months after my big move, I flew from New York to Los Angeles on a plane packed with baby G.I.s. They were handsome and bright-eyed, their uniforms crisp and new. None of them could have been more than twenty-one. When they got to their base on the West Coast, they told me, they'd find out whether they were going to be deployed to Vietnam or Germany. Understandably, they all wanted to go to Germany.

One of the boys I remember in particular. With his dark, Italian eyes and Brooklyn accent, he charmed me from the start. I was still a kid myself at the time, barely twenty-one, but he seemed so young to me, so naïve. I imagined him stomping through the Vietnamese jungles, dirty and exhausted, his beautiful eyes glassy with shock. The image nearly broke my heart.

"I know a way for you to get what you want," I told him.

"Really?" His face lit up. "I'll try anything!"

I described the creative visualization process that Ron had taught me a few months before. Immediately, he and his friends pulled out notebooks and pens, and started writing out their desires, starting with "I am stationed in Germany." I think one of them wanted to meet a blond fräulein, too.

A month later, a letter was sent to my inflight office at J.F. Kennedy Airport. It was the G.I. from Brooklyn, thanking me. He'd been assigned to a base in Germany.

Imagination Equals Creation

Buddha said, "The mind is everything. What we think, we become."

Henry Ford put it a bit differently: "Whether you think you can, or you think you can't, you are usually right."

The power of the human imagination is unlimited. Sadly, it's also pretty much untapped.

No matter how old we get, or how much we think we know, our internal programming governs nearly every aspect of our lives—right up until the moment when we wake up and realize *we can make our own decisions.* We change our world by changing the way we think about our world. We are worthy, blessed, gorgeous, and abundant (or unworthy, cursed, ugly, and lacking) not because we were born that way, but because those are the thoughts by which we live.

When I was a kid, my parents told me over and over, "Rebecca, be realistic!" Reality, as we've been conditioned to know it, consists solely of the three-dimensional world. But as great spiritual teachers throughout the ages have taught, this reality isn't real at all; rather, it's a projection of our thoughts, feelings, and beliefs *about* our reality.

The mistake most people make is thinking that what they sense—what they can "prove"—is the whole of what exists. However, since every bit of information about the world is fed to them through the square holes of their subjective, human senses and the Rules programmed into their human minds, it too becomes subjective. True knowledge about ourselves and our reality cannot be gained through analysis of sensory input or any current paradigm of "reality."

This is the grand illusion, the magic trick we're all looking to unravel: if we are not our bodies, and we are not our sensory minds, then *who are we?*

In the realm where the true Self resides, there is no ego; no I, me, or mine. We are everything, and everything is us. There are no definitive parameters, no labels, no fixed forms, no beginnings, and no ends. There is no Time. This realm of infinite possibilities is the Fourth Dimension— the home of Universal Consciousness, the Ocean of the Absolute. This is where G.O.D. lives, and it is from this place that our consciousness can transform, transcend, and reshape this impermanent physical dimension.

In order to create using tools like Ron's visualization technique, you must first accept that the reality with which you're familiar *isn't real.* You aren't in the airplane; the airplane is in you.

I know what you're thinking: "How can the world I can see, touch, and taste be unreal? That makes no sense!" My answer to you is this: your world is as real as you make it. Every day when you wake up, you make a decision (consciously or unconsciously) to reiterate the thoughts and patterns of yesterday, or change them. You choose to stay in your relationship or leave it. You choose to feel good or bad. You choose to feed your fears or set them aside. You choose to follow The Rules or leave them behind.

If you're not happy with your current reality, look closely at what you believe about it. Everything you tell yourself about your reality will eventually become true.

I call the process of opening to imagination and taking control of your reality "waking up." People who are awake make choices about their realities consciously, every day. They know that they become what they think, and they shape their thoughts accordingly. On the other hand, those who are still "asleep" allow choices to be made for them by their subconscious and/or unconscious minds, which are programmed according to childhood experience, genetics, and The Rules. Instead of acting, they're reacting. They're constantly at the mercy of the circumstances and people around them, and the realities which those people are creating, consciously or unconsciously, for themselves. (If you've ever felt "sucked in" to someone else's life drama, you know exactly what I'm talking about.)

The path to awakening bridges the space between the physical plane and the Fourth Dimension. It exists in only one place: your own creative mind, more commonly known as your imagination.

As children, we're taught that imagination is something you outgrow—a sort of escapist crutch which must ultimately be set aside in favor of practicality and The Rules. By the time we reach our teens, media provides our only real connection to this rich mental realm. Novels, movies, and video games are considered acceptable links to "alternate" realities for grown-ups, but although some suspension of disbelief (to borrow the literary term) is necessary to engage with any such medium, living in someone else's imaginary world is not the same as creating your own.

Creative visualization works best when your imagination is fully engaged. Whatever you can imagine becomes possible. All the great innovators of history imagined their inventions before they were actually manufactured. Everything man has manifested in this physical world—starting with the wheel—began its existence as an idea in someone's mind. With practice, you'll be able to see, smell, feel, and hear your desired reality as clearly and fully as you sense the three-dimensional world your body inhabits. More importantly, you'll be able to *believe* in your new reality as strongly as a young child believes in his or her imaginary friends. (Before you get defensive, who's to say that your five-year-old's imaginary friends aren't real? The only thing that can be said with any accuracy is that those friends aren't real *to you!*)

Maria Montessori, José Silva, and other metaphysical people who have studied children figured out that, when they're very young (up to age four), children are naturally in touch with the Fourth Dimension. Ask a young child, "Where did you come from before you were here?" and you may get a full accounting of past lives or alternate realities. My nephew used to tell me about his life as an adult man in India. His brother talked about wearing muddy boots and feeling mice run around his feet. When he was three, he told me a story about jumping out of an airplane. He often asks his grandfather about his experiences in World War II; it's like they're comparing notes.

Up to the age of seven, most children believe in magic because they know, innately, that they can make things happen with the power of their minds. Between the ages of seven and twelve, the channel to the Fourth Dimension is slowly closed as magical ideas are painfully disproved by "reality"—but the pathways of creative thinking are still open. It has been documented that children who learn to solve problems creatively (aka, imaginatively) at this stage of development are far more likely to succeed later in life than those boxed into a more mundane curriculum of performance testing and memorization.

After puberty, the window of imagination closes even more. Teens are taught to rely on their five senses, and develop a more concrete perception of three-dimensional time and space. They also rely more heavily on The Rules (or their resistance to them) to define themselves and their lives. External things like clothing, cars, and the physical body start to matter more and more. By the time most people turn twenty-one, The Rules are entrenched, and imagination plays little to no role in their daily reality of work, relationships, and acquisition-driven behavior.

The prison of realism can encase our minds, but imagination gives us wings. When you begin your creative visualization practice, it's important to give yourself time to get your imagination back in shape. Like any skill, creativity gets rusty with disuse. You may feel like a child learning to ride a bike all over again. You might even need training wheels for a little while—like visual aids, soundtracks, or lists. Take up activities that stimulate your creative brain, like painting, writing, or playing an instrument. Feel as you engage in these activities that you can tap into all the possibilities of the Fourth Dimension.

When it comes to manifesting, experiment with small things first. If you want to see more of your friends, envision yourself in their company. The phone will soon start ringing. If you want a new car, a new dress, or a pair of high-end shoes, use Ron's technique to imagine how you'll feel when these things come into your life. They may not always show up in the way you envisioned, but they *will* show up. Of course, material items aren't really all that important—but that's why they make for good practice. If you don't have a specific goal or item in mind, simply conjure up feelings of contentment and gratitude each morning and night, and see what happens.

Many spiritual traditions will tell you that you're not supposed to use the power of the higher mind—the Fourth Dimension—to get stuff in this material realm. If anything, you're supposed to renounce material wealth and pretty things, and go live in a cave somewhere in the Himalayas with nothing but your loincloth and a couple of sacks of rice. I don't believe that at all. It's true that when you are happy and fulfilled, material possessions matter a lot less because you're no longer relying on external stuff for internal fulfillment. But the realm of matter exists as we create it, and when we call in abundance from a place of connection with G.O.D. and the higher self there's nothing wrong with receiving. When we are in alignment with G.O.D., there is no such thing as lack.

A Perfect Plan

When your job involves long stretches in the sky, you have a lot of time to read. After Ron taught me about creative visualization, I dove into every metaphysical book I could get my hands on. I read works by Napoleon Hill, George Ivanovich Gurdjieff, Shakti Gawain, and a host of other metaphysical teachers. Other Stews would ask me about my somewhat unorthodox reading material, and I would share with them what I learned.

One of my flying partners, Donna, was based with me at John F. Kennedy Airport in New York. She was working on a transfer back to her native California but struggling with the logistics. I taught her Ron's techniques and lent her some of my books.

A few months later, a letter was delivered to my New York apartment. "You'll never guess what happened!" Donna wrote. "I used your creative visualization techniques, and my transfer went through immediately. My father and brother had an apartment ready for me as soon as I moved. And, just before I left our station at Kennedy Airport, the supervisor came up to me and asked, 'How would you like to go into management?' You were right! All I had to do was visualize what I wanted and trust that it would work out. I truly feel that there is a perfect plan for me, and I'm living it right now!"

When our souls—our highest selves—choose to incarnate on this three-dimensional plane, it's usually because we have a job to do or a purpose to fulfill. Everyone, no matter what his or her circumstances, is here for a reason. Our highest selves have a plan, and it contains exactly what we need to grow and evolve into a spiritualized, loving, magical being.

This perfect plan is laid out in accordance with divine principles, which are not subject to the laws of the three-dimensional world. They are not even subject to those things we think of as absolute—like gravity, Time, or the physics of motion. They are the laws of the Fourth Dimension, the spiritual realm, and they supersede everything in the limited reality of this physical world.

One of the most important steps in waking up is to take responsibility for the reality you've created for yourself. Consciously or unconsciously, you've chosen the path of your existence because it coincides with your soul's perfect plan. That's it. No exceptions.

This is where the turbulence starts for most people. You might ask, "How can I be responsible for my trauma, my abuse, my failed marriage?" But in some way, you did choose those experiences, either because they perpetuated the underlying ideas you already had about your reality, or because they contained valuable lessons for your soul's development. Once you wake up, you can choose to shift your ideas, and therefore your experience—but while you're still asleep, you will keep running up against the same walls over and over.

I see this vicious cycle in people I know all the time. They get stuck in the same relationships, fall into the same depressions, hide from the same fears, over and over. They change the set, but they're still reading the same script. As painful as it is to watch (and to live), this is all part of the greater plan. Just like in a classroom, the same information will be presented over and over in different ways until the lesson is learned. Since our reality is merely a mirror of our thought, *our reality cannot change until our awareness shifts.*

However terrible the traumas of your past or the struggles of your present, you have the power to create change. Your perfect plan was created to move your soul forward toward greater understanding. In fact, once you acknowledge that your life is right now, at this moment, unfolding according to a larger plan, you rise above the rules of the mundane world and place yourself in alignment with the spiritual realm. In other words, you become a co-creator with G.O.D. and your highest self. Instead of following the plan, you *become* the plan.

Our programming tells us that there are things we must accept as intrinsic to the human condition. I disagree. We are not victims. Yes, the bodies we inhabit will eventually age and die. That's part of the plan; the changes we experience in the aging process help us grow. But when we're awake, there is very little else we can't shift with the power of our thought. We don't have to accept lack, illness, conflict, or suffering. We don't have to carry the burdens of fear, anger, or doubt. As long as our wills and imaginations are strong enough, and our minds open enough, we can reshape our reality to reflect G.O.D.'s divine principles of love, abundance, health, joy, oneness, and reciprocity.

Often, our human minds put up barriers that separate us from this divine reality. We judge others because we feel that we're being judged ourselves, or because we're afraid of being wrong. We withhold love because, deep down, we feel unworthy of love. We create partitions between "us" and "them," even though G.O.D. is universal and all-encompassing. The religions and Rules we were raised with may not recognize these separations as constructs of the sleeping human mind; in fact, they may actually encourage them. Same goes for popular culture. The mainstream media tells us that we need to be fearful of nearly everything: crime, disease, aging, weight gain, other cultures, our own neighbors, the food we eat, the water we drink, the air we breathe. With every new fear that is added, we retreat one step further into the shadows.

If we truly desire to move closer to G.O.D. and our own perfect plan, we must recognize and dismantle any thoughts which are not in alignment with the divine principles. Ultimately, *all suffering is a result of being out of alignment with the divine principles.*

Part of being awake is being vigilant. As Mary Baker Eddy wrote in *Science and Health with Key to the Scriptures*: "Stand porter at the door of thought. Admitting only such conclusions as you wish realized in bodily results, you will control yourself harmoniously." Freedom from separateness and misalignment comes only through self-knowledge. You have the power to control your thoughts; therefore, you hold the key to your own absolution.

Ultimately, any and all challenges presented to us during our time on Earth are intended to teach us. No matter how dire our circumstances, we are not being punished. When we wake up, we shift from "Why me" into "Why not!" Every new situation becomes a riddle to be unraveled, because underpinning each experience is the truth that we are not separate from G.O.D., and G.O.D. is not separate from us.

Stepping Up, Taking Charge

In the early part of the twentieth century, metaphysical teachers like Neville Goddard and Earl Shoaff urged people to become active in creating their own destinies. (The latter, coincidentally, was the uncle who taught my friend Ron the art of creative visualization.) Such empowerment teachings have grown in popularity since. But in many traditions, the prevailing attitude is still more passive: turn things over to God, and God will provide—or he won't, depending on how "good" you are and what kind of mood He's in.

In one sense, we do need to learn to surrender. After a point, you have to release control over your manifestations and trust that the things you desire will come to you in accordance with the divine principles and your own perfect plan. However, if you simply accept everything that comes into your reality without working on your own behalf, you're not aligning yourself with G.O.D.; rather, you are behaving like a student who refuses to study. I mean, you *could* try to get through college on the mantra, "If God wants me to do well on this test, I will," but you'll probably flunk out before your sophomore year. The school of life is no different. We are offered challenges so that we can learn and grow by them—not so we can meekly lie down and wait to be rescued.

According to Gregg Braden, author of *The God Code*, the words "God/Eternal Within the Body" are actually written on our DNA. Jesus preached, "The Kingdom of Heaven is within you." If you have a rich inner connection to G.O.D., you will always have the resources to reinvent yourself, redirect yourself, and remain connected and happy, no matter what zingers the physical world throws at you. But the moment you separate yourself from the Kingdom within, you slide out of the driver's seat. Who takes the wheel isn't God, or Jesus, but your own subconscious mind, with all of its embedded programming.

In other words, total surrender requires total clarity.

José Silva said in 1998 that we are entering the next phase of human evolution. The old structures of religion and three-dimensional science are no longer enough to contain what we are discovering. In order to continue to move forward, we need to stop looking outward and start looking inward. Metaphysics provides us with the tools to do just that. However, as I learned quite soon after my initial experiences with creative visualization, there is a lot more to waking up than simply identifying what you desire.

If you want your life to be a clear channel for divine Consciousness, the first step is to clear the detritus from your internal landscape and begin to create change on the subconscious levels where manifestation begins.

In other words, you've got to sort through your baggage.

CHAPTER THREE

Baggage

*"There's a luggage limit to every passenger on
a flight. The same rules apply to your life. You
must eliminate some baggage before you can fly."*

~ Rosalind Johnson

Someone once accused me of becoming a flight attendant simply to satisfy my own vanity. In a way, this was true: I loved the image of myself in those cute little skirts and jackets, with my flawless makeup and jaunty little scarf. But mostly, I just wanted to be able to check things out. I knew that there was more to life than what I could see from the ground.

But checking things out—I mean, really paying attention—was a lot harder than I first thought.

It was 1968. I'd been flying for a year but hadn't yet taken advantage of the free flight passes allotted to me as a stewardess. It was about time I gave myself a real vacation, I decided. After poring over a map of the Caribbean, I decided Saint Croix seemed like an appropriately glamorous place for a first escape, so off I went.

My first impression of that island was of vibrancy. There was so much color, so much light. Surrounded by brilliant bougainvillea and waving palm trees, gazing out over the blue-green ocean, I felt I had truly found paradise. I checked into the King Christian hotel in Christiansted, feeling incredibly lucky that my job afforded me deep discounts and special treatment at high-end places. I unpacked, slipped into my teensy-weensy bikini, and headed for the beach.

As I dug my toes into the sand, I sighed, waiting for that island tranquility to descend on me like a cooling rain. But it didn't happen. I couldn't relax.

At the time, life was coming at me from all directions. I felt like I was losing control. I had bounced a check paying my utility bill. In those days, there was no overdraft protection, and bouncing a check was a big deal. The electric company actually called my employer to find out if I would be able to cover the check. United Airlines didn't like that one bit, and told me that if they got another phone call from my bank, they would fire me.

Obviously, I had to get a better handle on my finances. I'd been too busy having fun to pay attention to my bank balance.

In addition, my apartment situation was up in the air. The beautiful apartment I'd manifested came with a major downside. In my manifestation, I hadn't asked for a *safe* place, just a beautiful, accessible, affordable one. A few months into our stay, Sara and I discovered that the manager of our building was stalking us.

This man—we'll call him Guy—would let himself into our apartment in the early hours of the morning and tiptoe into our bedroom. He must have been hoping to catch us naked, or in the middle of some naughty activity. The first time I woke up to find him standing over my bed I must have jumped a mile.

"Guy!" I gasped. "What do you want? Is everything okay?"

He didn't answer, just turned around and walked out, locking the door carefully behind him.

I was seriously confused. Despite my worldly job and know-it-all attitude, I was pretty naïve. The 1960s in general were a naïve time. Most of us just assumed that other people meant well. Maybe, I reasoned, there had been a break-in while I was off flying, and Guy was concerned for us. Maybe someone had reported a strange noise on our floor. Maybe he was tired and had simply wandered into the wrong apartment (even though his apartment was five floors away from ours).

But when the same creepy scenario kept happening, I realized that our building manager was a pervert. I started to imagine all the nasty things he was thinking while he stood over Sara and me in the night. Every time I saw him in the lobby, my guts went icy cold. I thought about telling someone, but I wasn't the kind of girl who went running for help. Nor was Guy the kind of person I wanted to set off. I needed to find my own solution.

So there I was in Saint Croix, with my body basking in the sun on a perfect tropical beach and my thoughts entrenched in the noise and grit of the Big Apple. As waves lapped the white sand a few feet away, my mind turned over scenario after scenario. What was happening back at the apartment? Was Sara okay? Was creepy Guy tossing my underwear drawer, or pawing through my uniforms? How was I going to find a new place to live if I was bouncing checks? I felt totally at the mercy of all these external forces, like a flower caught in a tornado.

As I fretted, a voice came to me out of the depths of my mind. *Leave New York in New York,* it said.

I blinked and sat up. It was like the proverbial light bulb had gone off in my head. I had left New York behind in body, but it was still with me in spirit. Worrying wouldn't accomplish anything. I was missing the beauty in front of me because I was obsessing about things that were happening more than a thousand miles away. If I was going to enjoy my first real vacation at all, I had to leave behind where I had been, and embrace where I was.

That day, I received one of the most important lessons of my life. The happiest travelers—on vacation or in life—are those who can be where they are, fully and completely. So many people are either stuck in the past or obsessing over the future. They're resting on their laurels, reliving past glories, or speculating about events that may never happen. I was one of the latter: my mind was a whirling storm of shifting possibilities, each one more awful than the last. Not only was I devoting the majority of my thoughts to situations that hadn't happened yet, I was feeding those thoughts with the energy of my fear and anxiety. Even worse, I was missing a positive experience because I was too busy creating a negative one in my head.

Then and there, I decided that nothing was going to get in the way of me enjoying myself. I was going to leave New York in New York, and have myself a grand old time.

The next day, I met a man in the bar of the King George Hotel. His name was Alan and he was a businessman from somewhere in the South—Alabama, maybe, or Mississippi. He owned a big yacht that had recently been used by *Playboy* as a location for a feature shoot. He was just about to head to Puerto Rico to pick up the yacht and sail it back to Saint Croix.

"You should come with me," he said, with a charming smile. "I have to make the trip anyway, and it would be fun to have company."

Naturally, I said yes.

It was a strange trip, but I enjoyed every minute of it. We flew to San Juan the next day. Before heading to the marina, we made a quick stop at the downtown office of Alan's friend. I don't remember the friend's name, but I have a clear mental snapshot of the enormous leopard named Pattycakes who lived in a cage in his waiting room. When we went out to dinner, the friend ordered his steak raw. Not rare, *raw*. The meat was practically still mooing— just the way Pattycakes would have liked it.

With my new determination to live in the moment, I took it all in stride.

We spent the night on the yacht. Alan was a perfect gentleman, and had a separate cabin made up for me. The next morning, we set sail for Saint Croix. If you've ever been sailing, you'll agree that it can be one of the most tranquil, even boring, experiences in creation. We floated across the gentle waves for two straight days, with nothing but ocean, sky, and the occasional bird to be seen.

When I wasn't chatting with Alan, I had plenty of time to think. At first, my mind wanted to snap back to the worrying and what-ifs, but I decided to employ my creative visualization techniques instead. As my focus shifted from problems to solutions, I felt the doors of possibility opening.

I said goodbye to Alan in Saint Croix with many thanks and a promise to call if I was ever in his neighborhood. On the way back to New York, I felt totally calm. I didn't have to live with Guy's skulking. My finances were completely under my control. There was nothing I couldn't handle because I *knew* I was in charge of my life. All I had to do was visualize a happier, healthier situation, and it would come into my reality.

Less than two weeks after my return, I got a phone call from my old college roommate. She was moving into an apartment on Sullivan Street in Greenwich Village, and wondered if I'd be interested in splitting the rent. I jumped at the opportunity. Sara was leaving in a few days for her hometown of Minneapolis; her boyfriend had been discharged from the Army, and wedding plans were in the works. The timing couldn't have been more perfect.

Now, I just had to deal with Guy.

Any time I needed a ride to or from the New York airports, I called the limo service contracted by United Airlines. I had befriended one driver in particular. I called him Charley Weaver, after the famous 1950s television character, because that's who he looked like—complete with bushy moustache, pot belly, and battered hat.

I told Charley about the situation with Guy, and he said, "You just let me know when, sweetheart, and I'll get you out of there."

He was as good as his word. When moving day came, he showed up with two burly driver buddies. The three of them cleared out my apartment in a snap. As the guys were hauling out my sofa, creepy Guy the manager came out of his hiding hole to shout at me.

"What do you think you're doing?" he howled. "You have a lease! You can't just walk out of here!"

"Watch me," I said.

"I'll see you in court! I have signed documents!" He was practically foaming at the mouth. Obviously, the idea that I was putting an end to his nightly peep show was too much for him to handle.

I stood on my tiptoes, and looked him straight in the eye. "You bet, Guy," I purred. "I'd *love* to see you in court."

He shrank away, and hurried back to his office. I never heard another peep out of him.

What Are You Carrying?

As Charley guided his limo expertly through the streets of Midtown with my couch strapped to the roof, I felt a huge burden lift from my shoulders—as though I'd been carrying a heavy bag, and I'd finally set it down.

Baggage is like that: heavy. The more fears, doubts, negative experiences, expectations, and other random crap we carry with us, the heavier life feels.

The way I see it, there are four kinds of baggage: physical, emotional, spiritual, and future (aka, expectations). Any one of them can slow you down. Combined, they can be like an iron ball and chain, dragging at you with every step.

The encouraging thing is that you get to choose your baggage. If there's something you don't want to bring along on your travels—negative or frightening experiences, past relationships, feelings of inadequacy or dependency—you can choose not to pack them. It's really that simple.

The first kind of baggage, physical baggage, is the easiest to understand. So many of us are attached to the stuff we own—and perhaps even more so to the stuff we don't yet have. A substantial chunk of our self-worth is based upon the quality, quantity, and dollar value of our physical possessions. I mean, what kind of person are you without your smartphone, your Coach bag, your Armani suit, or your red Louboutins?

The answer, of course, is, "The same person you are with them!" Stuff is just stuff. It exists purely in the physical plane. Stuff has no consciousness of its own; its only ties to the Fourth Dimension are the thoughts you hold about it. There's nothing wrong with having it, but when you can't put it down and walk away, it becomes baggage. If you can't let it go, it controls you.

Years ago, it was stylish to travel with a lot of luggage. Most of our first-class passengers were followed in and out of the airport by two or three porters, each pushing a mountain of matching cases. The more you carried with you, the more distinguished and important you were perceived to be. To some extent, this is still true, though it's a lot harder to travel with a train car's worth of luggage these days. Now, it's more about *what* you bring, and how nonchalant you can be about it.

In the early 1990s, an airline captain with whom I was friendly took his wife, Ida, on a vacation to Costa Rica. The country was just starting to gain a reputation as a tourist destination, and the captain had booked their stay at one of the most luxurious resorts on the Pacific coast.

A few months before their trip, the captain bought Ida a diamond ring. It must have been seven or eight carats, and it gleamed like a headlamp on her finger. Dying to show it off to her fellow vacationers (and afraid to leave it at home, lest the maid walk off with it), she wore it on their trip. I was working their flight, and I "oohed" and "aahed" appropriately, although privately I thought she was nuts to bring a ring like that to Central America.

Once they touched down in Costa Rica, Ida started to feel the first twinges of anxiety. I can't say for certain how much the ring was worth, but it was probably a year's salary for the average Joe. There was a safe in the hotel room, but it wasn't secure enough for her to feel comfortable leaving the ring there all day, so she wore the darned thing everywhere, even in the ocean. Whatever she was doing, a part of her mind had to be conscious of what was happening with the ring. Was it safe? Could those unsavory-looking guys over by the beach bar see it glinting in the sun? Would a barracuda bite it off her finger while she was snorkeling?

All that fear sent a very clear message to the universe. The first day, someone stole Ida's running shoes off the deck. The next day, her sunglasses went missing. Consumed with anxiety about the theft of her ring, Ida was attracting the very thing she feared. By the end of the vacation, she barely wanted to leave the hotel room. Everyone had seen her ring by then; how could they have missed it? Now, she was certain, the mysterious "they" were lurking in every dark corner, waiting to clobber her over the head with the nearest two-by-four and steal her precious diamond.

On the return flight, she confessed to me, "I've never been so glad to be done with a vacation. I'll never go anywhere like that again."

Now, this is an extreme example, and I'm fairly sure (although I can't say for certain) that fear was a major factor in other areas of Ida's life as well. But it goes to show you the damage that attachment to physical things can do to a person emotionally.

The irony, of course, was that the diamond was supposed to make Ida happy. Instead, it became a burden. The way she viewed her situation, and the people around her, was skewed and darkened by her fear of losing her shiny bauble. Those guys by the bar were probably perfectly nice people, just trying to have a good time—but to Ida, they were suspects in a future crime of indeterminate magnitude.

We are told by the media, our programming, and The Rules that material objects are supposed to make us feel happy and fulfilled. They say, "Look how hard

I worked! Look how much my husband loves me! Look how special/unique/deserving I am!" For people with a lot of material baggage, what they own becomes who they are—and if that's the case, what happens when their stuff gets damaged, lost, or grows old? How does that reflect on them?

The flip side of stuff is the lack of stuff. We desire shiny new cars, bigger and better homes (and stuff to fill them), designer clothes, the right products and cosmetics… The list goes on and on. The desire to acquire material possessions drives many of us to work harder, save more diligently, or spend more wantonly. We believe that when we have X, Y, and Z, our lives will be happier, easier, and more fulfilling. Deep down, we're not actually looking for more stuff, but a way to satiate our egos, and find a sense of relevance and security in the world.

Recently, I had a conversation with a friend that perfectly illustrates the damage that attachment to stuff can cause. This friend—we'll call him Dan—is at heart a nice guy, but he's a bit image-conscious. Over the decades, he's made it a point to use his stuff to prove his worth as a person. He drives a luxury sports car with a six-figure price tag. He lived in an enormous house with all the expected accoutrements—until his divorce, when he moved into an enormous carriage house and proceeded to outfit it like something out of *Better Homes and Gardens*. The most important thing, to him, is not that he's happy and content, but rather that other people perceive him as being happy and content. If ever there was a person who could keep up with the Joneses, Dan would be him.

Even in the midst of his divorce, he did splendidly at presenting the well-to-do façade. But then, the unthinkable happened: he lost his lucrative corporate job. Suddenly, there was no money lying around to pay for all that stuff he'd acquired—but he couldn't bring himself to tell his soon-to-be ex-wife and ten-year-old twins that circumstances had to change. Even as his unemployment benefits dwindled, he continued to support his family's extravagant lifestyle as if nothing was different.

When we had our conversation, he told me he felt that if he "checked out" of this life, he'd be happier. The stress of holding on to all of his possessions was literally killing him. His ego, unwilling to surrender, refused to let go of its attachments when circumstances called for change. Now, he was literally looking over the edge of a cliff.

"What if you sold your car?" I asked him. "Or put some furniture in a consignment shop?"

He looked at me as though I'd lost my mind. "No way!" he said. "That's all I have left!"

I find it amazing that some people would rather die than let go. I mean, you can't take your things with you when you die, so eventually you have to let them go anyway. Sure, you can have a good time with what you own, but gathering shiny toys isn't the point of life on Earth. All the advertising claims about "improved quality of life" are a crock. No dishwasher or LCD television is going to bring anyone bliss. In my experience, one of the surest ways to decrease your quality of life is to chase the material goods that claim to hold the key to it.

Dan's situation is a difficult one, but it's not a dead end. By equating his lifestyle with who he is as a person, he's creating his own hell on earth—one from which he believes death is the only escape. The key to his liberation lies in recognizing that even if he has to sell his sports car, move into a smaller apartment, and buy his clothing in a thrift store, *he will still be the same Dan.* His fourth-dimensional self will still be fully intact and connected to G.O.D. Only his ego will be hurt.

The more time and energy we devote to objects in the material realm, the less we have to devote to what really matters—things like love, truth, imagination, and creativity, all of which exist in the Fourth Dimension. If your attention is focused on acquiring, preserving, and evaluating stuff, there's not a lot of time left over for soul-searching. The more baggage you carry with you, the more diversions you have. The more diversions you have, the more barriers you unconsciously erect between your real, fourth-dimensional self and your temporary, physical self. Conversely, the less you have to worry about in the way of worldly goods, the more you can free your mind to make a connection to G.O.D. This is why some people choose to live in ashrams and monasteries. With the temptation to attach to extraneous stuff no longer muddying the waters, they can see more clearly to the bottom of their wells.

Of course, you need a certain amount of stuff to get by in the world. Almost everyone—even a monk—needs a roof overhead, food to eat, a bed to sleep in, and clothing to keep warm. But after that, it seems we're subject to the law of diminishing returns. Will you truly be happier if you eat your food off fine china, instead of a plain, simple plate? It's still food, and it's still nourishing. Does it matter if you sleep under your grandmother's old quilt or a designer down coverlet? You're warm either way. Again, I'm not saying that it's wrong to have nice things, or even to want nice things. What is harmful is when those things cover or replace your true identity—when you find yourself lugging around a bag so heavy you can barely lift it, for no better reason than you can't bear to let your stuff out of your sight.

Buying Into the Illusion

I've always liked to travel light. I once had a fantasy that someone would design a line of disposable paper clothing. When I was done wearing something, I could simply tear it off and throw it away (or even better, recycle it). When I was flying, I loved to toss out old clothes in various places around the world. There was nothing more satisfying to me than returning from a trip with a suitcase that felt lighter than when I left. Every time I got rid of something, I felt my mental burden get that much lighter, too.

My first real experience with putting stuff before substance was in the early 1970s. I was flying to Tokyo to meet a new boyfriend, and decided that I was going to go in style. To that end, I spent a bundle on a beautiful Gucci suitcase. Strutting through the airport with this glittery, glamorous bag in my hand, I felt like a movie star. I couldn't wait to show my superficial businessman beau my newest acquisition. I mean, who *wouldn't* want a girl who totes her stuff in a Gucci bag?

I fixed my makeup in the airplane bathroom before we landed, and straightened out my clothes. I looked like a million bucks. But when I retrieved my luggage, I was in for quite a shock. My beautiful Gucci bag came off the conveyor belt looking like it had been through a war. It was torn, filthy, and nearly ruined. Plus, the zipper was broken!

The "designer quality" everyone raved about was a load of crap. I'd spent hundreds of dollars on an illusion.

The man I was seeing, Robert, met me at the airport in the company of one of his business associates, a man named Rokomoto. Robert introduced me as "a prominent American television personality." I guess he was embarrassed to be dating a mere stewardess. I was shocked, but played along, maneuvering myself so I stood in front of my ruined suitcase.

"Nice to meet you, Rokomoto San," I said in my chirpiest voice. "You've got a great face for television."

Needless to say, Rokomoto and I hit it off immediately. He barely glanced at my torn-up bag as he hoisted it into the limousine. Thanks to Robert and his lies, I had something even more glittering than Gucci to show off in Tokyo.

I kept up the pretense for the rest of the trip. I didn't want to let Robert down, or make him look like a jerk in front of his client. In a way, it was fun to be someone else for a while. But deep down, I knew that what I was doing was totally out of alignment. I was putting up a front, making *stuff*—in this case, my invented job—more real than who I actually was.

In other words, I was buying into the illusion.

Metaphysical people know that, when you're connected to the Fourth Dimension, everything you need to be healthy, happy, and productive in this physical plane will show up. If you lose your stuff, more stuff will appear. Many practitioners I know make it a point to get rid of their possessions periodically, so that new and better things can come into their experiences. Paring down to the essentials can be very liberating. The act of letting go allows your true self to come to the forefront. Think of all you could experience if your stuff wasn't tying you down!

As consuming as it is, though, what you own is just one aspect of physical baggage. There's also the body you walk around in. Just like your stuff, it exists only in the physical world. José Silva used to describe the body as a spacesuit, and I agree. My human body is necessary to perform all the tasks I need to do on this plane, so I should be careful to take good care of it. But this body is not who I am.

To identify too strongly with the body can be really harmful. You can do as many sit-ups as you want, but will your six-pack abs make you a kinder, more compassionate person? Not necessarily. In some cases, striving for physical perfection can have the opposite effect, encouraging rigidity, anxiety, and judgmental tendencies—all of which create barriers rather than tearing them down.

Again, our programming plays a big part. Many women hold a core belief that if they aren't beautiful, they aren't lovable. The media and the beauty industry know this, and take full advantage of our insecurities. Again, I'm not saying that looking good is a bad thing. I love makeup as much as the next girl, and haven't missed a salon appointment in years. But this body is just a suit my soul is wearing. It changes, ages, and shifts—but nothing that happens to my body can affect the true me unless I allow it. The minute my identification with my body gets in the way of my connection with my highest self, it becomes baggage.

The Invisible Bag of Bricks

Spiritual leader Morrnah Nalamaku Simeona said, "If we can accept that we are the sum total of all past thoughts, emotions, words, deeds and actions and that our present lives and choices are colored or shaded by this memory bank of the past, then we begin to see how a process of correcting or setting aright can change our lives, our families and our society."

Robert Holden, PhD., wrote, "Sometimes, in order to be happy in the present moment, you have to be willing to give up hope for a better past."

A friend once said to me, "Some things, you never get over." My response was, "Well, as long as you think you won't, you won't."

All of us carry experiences, memories, and physical scars from our pasts. Having varied and intense experiences in the world is part of being alive. The situations we encounter are tests administered in life's classroom by our higher selves or G.O.D. In order to pass, we have to learn the lesson that is being presented. If the lesson isn't learned to our soul's satisfaction, we're forced to take the test again. And again. This is how people end up in the same financial quandaries, the same abusive relationships, the same dependent friendships, over and over again. These people aren't doomed to a life filled with suffering by some vengeful deity; they simply aren't passing their tests. Maybe they haven't even figured out that they're being tested.

Our experiences in the world can be both positive and negative, but the negative ones seem to leave the deepest imprints on the psyche. The Rules say that you have to hang on to past experiences—that they shape you like cookie molds. We may hate our memories, even run from them—but on a deeper level, we cling to them like security blankets, thinking that our suffering defines us. We label ourselves as abuse victims, cancer survivors, battered women, business failures. If you're stuck in the three-dimensional world of matter and The Rules, these definitions have weight—but in the Fourth Dimension, where G.O.D. lives, there is no such thing as suffering. There are only lessons, which we can choose to learn, or to ignore, as we like. When you're really tuned in, saying "I'm a victim" makes about as much sense as saying, "I'm an algebra test." You aren't the test. You are a divine being who is trying to learn from the test.

I'm not trying to be glib, but sometimes, when you're turning the magnifying glass on your emotional baggage, it helps to cultivate a little perspective. You are not a product of your circumstances. You are not even a product of your thoughts about your circumstances. *You are a divine being experiencing the reality your thoughts and your perfect plan have created.*

The traumas and terrors to which we cling represent our unlearned lessons. They are like bricks, and your mind is like a bag. The more bad stuff you carry, the heavier your mind feels. These bricks are not the building blocks of your personality; they don't support you in the least. They are merely a wall behind which you hide your true, divine self. The more bricks you carry, the harder it can be to show who you really are, and receive the gifts of love, joy, and divine abundance which are your birthright.

As I said, your bricks represent unlearned lessons. When you learn the lesson, you can toss away the brick. Sometimes this is a slow process, unfolding over the course of months or years. The brick slowly crumbles into dust, until you barely recognize it as the same brick that weighed you down for so long. Other times, it happens all at once—a sort of spontaneous enlightenment. When you fully realize the truth of your divine nature, you can simply set down your bricks and walk away. (It's not a coincidence that the word "enlightenment" contains the word "lighten." When we lighten our mental load, we become more enlightened!)

As you sort through your bricks, you'll begin to see that there are different levels to understanding. Freud and Jung weren't wrong; childhood suffering and our relationships with our parents explain a lot about how and why we do things. But traditional psychology falls short when it comes to releasing baggage. Identifying the cause of something is only half the work. Maybe your mother's lack of affection causes you to distrust every woman in your life—but does that mean you're stuck with that pattern forever? Of course not! Rather than simply saying, "This is who I am"—rather than creating another brick to carry—you can move beyond the cause to create a different effect.

You can recognize the lessons you learned from the old experience, and choose a new one.

My personal technique is to say to myself, "I am not my body, I am not my mind." I say this every morning when I wake up, and every night before I go to sleep. It's a reminder to my unconscious mind that the world I perceive with my five senses is not the beginning and end of my existence. I am more than the sum total of my memories and experiences. I am a divine being in a human spacesuit, on a mission to explore, through humanness, this incredible life on Earth.

Besides physical and emotional baggage, there are other kinds of baggage as well. Attachments to people, relationships, or romantic figures; celebrity worship; extreme patriotism; fears and phobias; even anxiety and depression can all be forms of baggage. It can be challenging and painful to examine our attachments to these things. It is easier to allow them to have power over us than to claim our power over them. But by clinging to narrow definitions of ourselves, or by making our self-definitions permanent and irrefutable, we create obstacles to growth. Fear is the mortar that holds our bricks in place.

Have you noticed that most people hate change? This isn't because change is bad, but because change is *hard*. It requires learning new lessons, letting go of old habits, and releasing unhelpful thought patterns and baggage. The human mind is inextricably connected to the ego, and the ego's purpose is to preserve itself. Being comfortable with change requires the realization that *you are not your ego*. You are not your body, and you are not your mind. There is nothing to fear in this world, because the real you—the you that is eternal and divine—is not of this world.

Our fourth-dimensional selves are eternal, so really, we have eternity to sort out who we really are—but patience isn't the same as inaction. Think of all of the excuses you invented as a teenager to get out of going to school. I know I got pretty creative when I needed a beach day. The mind— by which I mean the third-dimensional, human mind— doesn't like to let go of that habit of procrastination. It will generate excuse after excuse to hold on to its bricks, and to stay out of the classroom where life's harder lessons are learned. But how many times do you want to take the same test? How much suffering are you willing to endure before you take responsibility for your baggage?

CHAPTER FOUR

The French Twist

(It's Not My Problem)

"No problem can be solved from the same

level of consciousness that created it."

~ Albert Einstein

O nce you've uncovered your physical, emotional, and spiritual baggage, and repacked it in a way that serves you, you'll feel great. Having set down that proverbial bag of bricks, your whole being will feel lighter.

And then, someone will do something that really pisses you off.

The thing about relationships—personal, professional, or circumstantial—is that they don't just involve you and your stuff. They also involve other people and their stuff—and sometimes, their stuff is way out of control. Their bag of bricks has gotten so heavy that they can't carry it anymore, so they start flinging bricks at you, trying to lighten their load.

I remember one instance in particular when someone really let his bricks fly. I was working a non-stop flight from New York to Tokyo. As usual, I was thrilled to be traveling, and even happier to be working in first class, where the service was more intimate and I had time to chat with interesting people.

The other stewardesses and I were taking coats and getting passengers settled in their seats when a man cleared his throat behind me. I put a smile on my face and turned around, thinking he wanted a mimosa or a cup of coffee. (First-class fliers aren't noted for their patience.)

"Your French twist is crooked," the man said. He was average-looking, probably in his late forties, wearing a nicely tailored suit. His eyes were narrowed to mean little slits.

I was taken aback, but brightened up my smile and asked, "Which way is it crooked?"

"It's just crooked. You look sloppy."

I'll admit I had a flash of insecurity. I thought I was looking pretty fabulous that day. Had I missed something? And what did he mean, sloppy? Was my lipstick smeared? Did I have a run in my pantyhose?

As we prepared for takeoff, the man kept heckling me. He was determined to make me react. I refused to oblige, which only made him angrier. Through snark and snipe, I remained as cool as a cucumber. I felt like I was floating above his anger, just like the airplane would soon be cruising above the clouds.

What he couldn't know was that I'd recently had a revelation that changed the way I interacted with passengers, the rest of the crew, and everyone in my life.

For a long time, I held the view that my experience of life was dictated in some part by the people who shared it with me. Quantum physicists might call this entanglement; I'll call it "commingled baggage." I always hoped, especially on long flights, that interesting people would show up to amuse me. When they didn't, I'd be disappointed. When people complained or shouted in the cabin, I took it to heart—as though I needed to give more, do more, be more. I expected everyone to be satisfied with my work, all the time. If they weren't, I perceived it as a reflection on me.

In other words, I was carrying a lot of emotional baggage with me on the job.

One typical day in the sky, as I pushed the beverage cart down the aisle in economy class, serving Cokes and ginger ales in plastic cups, passengers on both sides of the aisle started tugging on my skirt and jacket to get my attention. Three or four kids screamed simultaneously. Some guy made a snarky comment about the "bimbos" who were working this flight. All of a sudden, I was on sensory overload in the middle of a snake pit. My brain kept shoving thoughts against the back of my throat. "Who do these people think they are? I'm only one person! I can only do so much!"

Stories about stewardesses who have had total breakdowns mid-flight are always circulating around the airline community. Out of the blue, a perfect Suzie Stew suddenly morphs into a human thunderstorm, screaming at the passengers, throwing things around the cabin, or crying hysterically. I'd always wondered how such a thing could happen to a perfectly normal girl—but now, I understood. I also knew that if something didn't shift very, very soon, I was going to be the next big sky gossip feature: Hurricane Rebecca.

I closed my eyes and drew a deep breath, praying to God to get me the hell out of there. All of a sudden, I was lifted right out of my body. A vision of Mother Teresa, tending to the poor in the gutters of Calcutta, flickered across my mind-screen. As those desperate, wounded people tugged at her hands and ankles, or clung, frightened, to her robes, she didn't scowl or brush them off. No, she tended to each of them in turn, nurturing them, loving them despite their despair.

Suddenly, I saw the passengers on that flight as those poor residents of Calcutta: needy, clutching, demanding. I could choose to hate them, and see them as impediments to my enjoyment of the situation—or I could nurture them patiently, do what I could to make them comfortable, and see them simply as... people.

I floated back down into my body, and exhaled my breath in a rush. Filled with compassion, I felt a smile spread over my face. Every person in that cabin was a person just like me. No better, no worse. They all had their own baggage, their own fears, their own anger. But none of their stuff had the power to affect me *unless I allowed myself to be affected.*

After that day, I was never again in danger of having a public meltdown. In fact, I became the go-to gal for advice about how to deal with troublesome passengers.

A few months later, I was working the first-class cabin with Sergio, a seriously handsome male flight attendant from Brazil. He was a hit with the ladies—so much so that flirty feminine attention often escalated into harassment. On this particular flight, a group of middle-aged matrons were running him around, giggling into their champagne and making crude jokes about pool boys.

"Am I just supposed to take this?" he fumed to me in the galley. "I am not a slave!"

"You don't have to sink to their level of unpleasantness," I told him. "You can feel however you want. It's your choice to stay above it."

Sergio blinked. "It is, isn't it?"

"Yes, I promise. *You* know you're not a boy toy. Who cares what they say?"

He flashed me a winning smile, and, holding his head high, swaggered back into the cabin. For the rest of the flight, although the ladies continued to squawk and giggle, nothing could shake his calm. Before I knew it, he was sharing my advice with all of our cabin-mates.

Flash forward to that Tokyo-bound flight. My attitude had been completely reprogrammed by my vision of Mother Teresa, and despite my brief flash of insecurity around the French twist comment, I knew that this guy simply wasn't capable of rocking my boat.

Finally, fed up with my nonchalant responses to his taunts, Mr. Jerk crooked his finger, beckoning me closer until our faces were just inches apart. "I'm going to have you in tears by the time this flight takes off," he hissed.

I studied him for a moment. I knew this couldn't be about me. In Stew school, they taught us that animosity from passengers was often generated by events totally beyond our control—beyond, more often than not, the confines of the airplane. We might remind someone of his ex-wife or a hated cousin. Our confidence might strike a chord with an insecure woman and cause her to lash out. You just never knew what could set someone off. But, in a sudden flash of insight, I knew what the trigger was for this guy.

"So, what happened to you this morning?" I asked. "Did you have a fight with your wife?"

My intuition was spot on. My questions took the fight right out of him. Yes, he'd had a fight with his wife. In fact, they hadn't gotten along for several years. Like a criminal who has just signed a confession, the man's aggression and defensiveness melted into relief and resignation. By seeing past the bricks he was flinging, I gave him permission to let go of his anger, and the shift was startling. For the rest of the flight, he was perfectly calm, even pleasant. By the time we disembarked in Tokyo twelve hours later, I found myself almost liking the guy—even as I double-checked my perfectly straight French twist in the bathroom mirror.

It's amazing how many of our daily interactions are colored by baggage. Sometimes, the only way to avoid being knocked down by flying bricks is to step out of ego completely, and into the far-seeing, compassionate space of the spiritual mind. Recognizing yourself as a spiritual, fourth-dimensional being is integral to happiness and contentment, because when you live from that place, no one else's baggage can weigh you down. You have supreme control over your feelings and reactions.

This sounds simple, but it's rarely easy. We tend to perceive each of our experiences subjectively, since the fourth-dimensional mind is shrouded by layers of ego, fear, anger, and judgment. "Well, how do you think that makes *me* feel?" is a sentence I hear a lot. My response is usually, "However you choose to feel."

Generally, when people lash out, it's not a reflection of the recipient (you), but rather of the burden of their own baggage. In other words, it's their problem, not yours. If you choose to make it your problem... Well, that's your problem.

I used to fly with a man whom the other Stews called Captain Hell. This guy was an airline legend. He was great at his job, but no one wanted to work with him because he radiated negativity like a bonfire radiates heat. As captain, he had the power to give direct orders to the rest of the flight crew, and took every opportunity to remind us of that power. He was controlling, arrogant, rude—at times, even cruel.

On one flight, I was standing by the cockpit door when the co-pilot stormed out, red-faced and shaking with fury.

"If he doesn't shut up, I'm going to strangle him!" he hissed. "Can *you* do anything with him?"

"I'll try," I promised, and slipped into the cockpit.

At first, I just made small talk. I figured if I could get the captain to chat about little things, he might loosen up enough to be tolerable. I was more right than I knew. Ten minutes into the conversation, he didn't just loosen up— he opened the floodgates.

As I stood there, dumbfounded, Captain Hell poured out what must have been years of repressed feelings about his unhappy marriage. He worked hard and made good money, but his wife didn't appreciate him. He was sick of coming home to a cold, sterile house. He was tired of the way she picked fights with him. But he couldn't tell her how he was feeling, because if he drove her to a divorce, she would take him to the cleaners.

These revelations showed Captain Hell in a whole new light. Rather than the Grendel of the sky, the Captain was nothing more than an extremely frustrated man. His lack of control on the ground had made him a legendary control freak in the air. His bag of bricks had turned into his defense mechanism, and it was a formidable weapon.

I wasn't responsible for his bricks. His bad home life was no one's fault but his own. He was the one who chose to stay put in a miserable situation. Afraid to lose his physical baggage—his money, his house, his trinkets—he was accumulating mental baggage at a staggering rate.

"I'm sorry things are so tough for you," I told him. "I know you'll find a way to make it better."

Captain Hell snapped his mouth shut, as if he'd only just realized that he was pouring out his heart to a woman he barely knew—and a lowly Stew at that. That famous scowl took up residence on his face once more, but it was a little softer than before.

After we landed, the co-pilot pulled me aside. "Whatever you did in there, it worked. Thanks a lot!"

"Just be nice to him. He's got a lot going on."

Like Ida with her ring in Costa Rica, our experiences are constantly filtered through whatever fear, anger, or ego-related baggage we're carrying, and our reactions to those around us shift accordingly. The great thing is that, once we become aware of these filters, we can choose to turn them off. With each filter we disassemble, each brick we unload, we get to move up a grade in life's classroom.

Another amazing fact is that we can actually control the energetic vibration of any environment in which we find ourselves *if we are in control of our reactions*. After my vision, I noticed that passengers weren't nearly as testy or demanding with me as they were with other stewardesses. It was as if they sensed that their bricks were just bouncing back at them. One-sided drama is no fun. Nothing they did could rile me up, so they stopped trying.

Eventually, my interactions in the cabin became a game to me. How much positivity and harmony could I create simply by maintaining my inner serenity? How many emotional bombs could I diffuse in the course of a trip? How long could I maintain that state of flow and higher consciousness before something pulled me out of it?

Michael Jackson, the late King of Pop, used to say that he was happier on stage than off. He just felt more like himself in his performer's clothes. It was the same for me. I was serene in the air, but for some reason, it was harder for me to maintain a high vibration on the ground in New York. Little life dramas would creep in and tackle me, and I would be back to my old, unenlightened ways of thinking, battered by other people's baggage and tossing my own bricks here, there, and everywhere. Only when we cleared the runway and took to the sky could I take a deep breath and relax.

Don't Take It Personally

In the Fourth Dimension, there are no barriers between us and other souls. We are not islands in an energetic void, separated by skin and space; rather, like strands in a universe-sized spider web, we are all linked to one another through divine Consciousness, and anchored by our connection to the divine laws of love, truth, health, and abundance. It's natural for our human minds to react when someone else throws a tantrum and shakes the web—but just because someone is caught in a personal earthquake doesn't mean we have to run for shelter.

In his book, *The Four Agreements*: *A Practical Guide to Personal Freedom,* Don Miguel Ruiz sets out four cardinal rules for operating in a space of happiness, abundance, and peace. Agreement #2 is titled, "Don't take anything personally."

He writes:

> *Nothing others do is because of you. What others say and do is a projection of their own reality, their own dream. When you are immune to the opinions and actions of others, you won't be the victim of needless suffering.*

Just as the Tokyo-bound businessman funneled years of anger about his failing marriage into an attack on my French twist, so will every person act and react from the center of his or her own individual reality. If that reality is positive and fulfilling, he will act and react in the "web" from a place of positivity and fulfillment. If his reality is negative, however, all his actions and reactions will come from that place of anger, fear, anxiety, or pain.

Therefore, when it comes to relationships, it's best to take Mr. Ruiz's Agreement #2 to heart. People will do what they do, but *it's your choice whether or not to suffer for it*. This is true whether you're the victim of road rage or rape, petty antagonism or outright abuse.

"Oh, sure," you say. "That's great, if you're talking about a nasty coworker or some random jerk on a plane. But what happened to me was so much worse. How can I possibly choose not to suffer when my father beat me, my mother hated me, my teacher molested me?"

Clearly, many of us have suffered terrible things, and learned some hard lessons in life's classroom. Through what seemed like no fault of our own, we were pulled into the twisted, hurtful reality of someone else, and our physical selves bear the imprint of that experience. However, nothing which is done to the physical body or the third-dimensional human mind can touch the pure essence of who you are—your fourth-dimensional self, which is part of G.O.D. That divine essence can be obscured or clouded by fear, anger, and pain, but all of those barriers are temporary, and can be cleared away by shifting your thought. This life is like Las Vegas: what happens in this dimension stays in this dimension.

I can attest to this personally because I was raped. Twice.

The first rape happened just a week after my graduation from Stew school. I was staying at a hotel at Chicago's O'Hare airport while I searched for an apartment. I felt glamorous and special with my brand new complimentary makeover, spotless fly suit, and hot-stuff attitude.

The hotel where I and my fellow sky goddesses were staying happened to be the same one where the pilots stayed during their layovers. We were ready to cut loose after six weeks of being cooped up in Stew school with our house mother—and the pilots knew it.

One captain (his initials were B.J., so that's what we'll call him) set his sights on me right away. He was probably in his mid-thirties; not gorgeous, but attractive enough. He sidled up to me in the hotel bar.

"Why don't you come up to my room for a drink?" he asked. "Bring your friends if you want."

This wasn't necessarily a proposition; a lot of crew members threw impromptu parties in their hotel rooms. Buying booze in the duty-free shops saved on "entertainment" costs. Plus, I was sure that a captain with a decade of experience in the sky would have lots of neat stories to tell. I practically jumped out of my seat with excitement.

"Sure," I chirped. "I'd love to!"

We went upstairs and joined a soirée which was already well underway. I had a couple of drinks, and was feeling a little sleepy and unsteady—but I was *not* going to miss out on my first real airline party. I accepted a third glass of champagne.

When I stood up to go to the bathroom, B.J. took my arm, and guided me away from the gathering. "Come here," he whispered. "I want to show you something."

Naïve and tipsy, I let him lead me into the bedroom. He closed the door behind him, leaving us in the dark. Then, he started kissing me.

At first, I was into the kiss. During Stew school, the Notre Dame college boys came to take us out on weekends—but they weren't like the pilots, with their manly aura of power and competence. It was kind of a rush to have this older man so interested in me, even before I'd had a chance to prove myself in the air.

Within a few minutes, it was clear that B.J. wanted more than just "petting," as we called it in those days. I froze. Suddenly, I wanted nothing more than to get away from him—but every time I tried to push him away, he pulled me back. When things started getting rough, I just stopped fighting. It was almost like I detached from my body and went somewhere else.

I know some people wouldn't call this rape, because I didn't kick him in the balls or scream for help, but in those days, it was common practice to lay the blame on the woman in situations like mine. Five decades ago, there were no such things as sexual harassment laws or corporate behavioral policies. Fortunately, the world has changed a lot since then—but at the time, there were no support structures for women in my situation.

The cold reality of what was happening raced through my head as the captain forced himself on my body. I'd gone up to his room; I'd downed those glasses of champagne. Everyone had witnessed him leading me away. If I filed a complaint, it would be B.J.'s word against mine—the accomplished captain against the baby Stew. If I squeaked, I would lose my position as a stewardess before I even got started, and there was no way I was going to let this creep ruin my flying career.

So I shut up and took it, literally.

They'd warned us in Stew school about certain pilots' predatory attitudes, but that night really put me on high alert. I studied the way the captains interacted with the other Stews, and saw exactly how I'd fallen for B.J.'s ploy. It really pissed me off—but even back then, before I'd gained any real metaphysical knowledge, I knew it was my choice to hang onto my bad experience, or let it go. B.J.'s inability to hear the word "No" had no power to make me feel worthless, dirty, or used; only I had that power.

I realize now that my reaction was a bit unusual.

Another girl from my graduating class, whom we'll call Lana, was also raped that year. Her situation was similar to mine in many ways. She met a man by the hotel pool during a daytime layover, and started chatting with him. She invited him back to her room for a drink, meaning the invitation literally—but apparently, he thought she was offering more. By the time push came to shove, he wouldn't take no for an answer.

I don't know what charges were filed, if any. But a few weeks after the attack, Lana left the sky for good, unable to overcome the fear that gripped her every time she set foot in a hotel room.

I was shocked to hear that she'd quit. Flying had been her dream. In school, we spent hours fantasizing about the places we wanted to explore, the people we wanted to meet. A few months before, we'd been working the same flight when our DC-6 came within mere yards of a smaller propeller plane in mid-air. Even that near-disaster hadn't dampened her enthusiasm.

It always seems disproportionate to me when a single negative hour in a person's life is granted the power to profoundly shape the hundreds of thousands of hours which come after it. Even the biggest bell, once rung, falls silent after a while—unless you keep ringing it.

Please don't think I'm being uncompassionate; I can absolutely understand why Lana reacted as she did. Fear is easy to create, and hard to escape. But we *do* have the power to overrule it. Human beings are not entirely creatures of instinct. Our third-dimensional minds like to hang on to experiences and feelings as anchors, or baselines—ways in which we can assess future situations without actually experiencing them. However, this is very rarely helpful in terms of spiritual growth. Our work is to become *less* reactive to this third-dimensional world, not more. With discipline, compassion, and understanding, we can begin to allow our fourth-dimensional minds to choose what our human minds hang on to, and what they let go. We can create new instincts, and erase even our most painful memories.

After my encounter with Captain B.J., I was more cautious around the pilots, but that didn't stop me from having a good time. I still went wherever I wanted, and did whatever seemed fun. It was that attitude that put me in my second sticky situation.

This time, there was no gray area: it was rape.

In 1966, a couple of years before I took to the sky, Air Jamaica celebrated its inaugural flight. Two years later, the Air Jamaica bigwigs offered free flight passes to United employees as part of a plan to promote the fledgling airline. Of course, I couldn't turn down such a grand opportunity, so I collected my friend Susie and took off for a three-day beach vacation.

We stayed at the Montego Beach Hotel, which was a pretty swanky joint. As soon as our bags were unpacked, we put on our spiciest bikinis and hit the beach.

If you've ever been to Montego Bay, you'll know that tourists are prime targets. Being young and cute, Susie and I were immediately set upon by the "beach boys"—lovely, dreadlocked Jamaican men who made a living taking tourists out on Sunfish sailboats and teaching them to surf.

These were independent contractors, not hotel employees, but they seemed nice enough, and most of the other hotel guests were middle-aged and (we thought) boring.

One of the beach boys—we'll call him Sean—took a particular liking to me. He kept circling around, trying to get me to go off with him.

"If you do not see the mountains before you go back to America," he told me, "You will be very disappointed."

I couldn't resist the lure of an adventure. I climbed up behind him on his moped, and off we went.

After a long climb up a dirt road lined with banana trees, we pulled over in front of a small shack. An older woman in an apron came out to meet us. Sean introduced her as his mother.

I was a bit taken aback—I had been expecting a tour, not a family meet-and-greet—but Mama Sean was sweet and friendly, and I found myself feeling happy that I hadn't missed this opportunity to stray off the beaten path.

"We can't stay long," Sean told his mother. "I am going to show Rebecca the good beach."

She looked from him to me, and back again. "You be careful, Sean," she said.

Looking back, I think she knew her son was up to something. But she didn't clarify her comment, and soon we were back on the moped, speeding toward the coast.

The "good beach" was better than good; it was incredible. At the end of a tricky climb down steep cliffs, we stepped onto a wide, horseshoe-shaped swath of pure white sand. Aqua waves broke gently over an offshore reef.

We walked along the beach. Sean was very quiet, but I was too busy taking in my surroundings to notice. When we were well away from the entrance, he grabbed my arm, spun me around, and started kissing me.

I pushed him off. "What are you doing?"

"You do not want me?"

"No! I want you to take me back to the hotel." He was so much bigger than I was. How had I not noticed?

He grabbed me again, harder this time. "You do what I say," he told me. "Or it will not be good for you."

He threw me down to the sand, and ripped off my bikini bottom.

Just like in the hotel room with Captain B.J., I found myself oddly detached. Every thought was logical and precise. There wasn't a soul around, so screaming wouldn't do me any good. I hadn't told anyone at the hotel where we were going, because I hadn't known. It would be hours before they even started to worry. If I didn't struggle, if I went along with what Sean wanted, there was a chance I would make it out of here. But if I fought him, he might hurt me, even kill me.

As my mind further separated itself from my body, I created the fantasy that Sean was my boyfriend. We were making love in the sand on a secluded beach, like any happy couple might. He wouldn't hurt me; he cared about me. That crazy sheen in his eyes was just the glimmer of passion...

After it was over, he pushed himself off me and stepped back into his shorts. I felt bruised and raw, and there was sand in places I don't want to mention. I stumbled to the edge of the water and washed myself, then reclaimed my bikini bottom from where he'd tossed it.

Sean beamed at me. He looked calm and relaxed, as though nothing untoward had happened. "Ready to go?" he asked.

I nodded. We walked back to the path, climbed up the cliff, and got on his moped. My skin crawled where I had to touch him.

"I will show you more," he called over his shoulder to me as we sped along.

"I should get back to the hotel," I replied, keeping my voice calm. "Susie will be wondering where I am."

"Oh, yes. We should not worry your friends. But you will be back here soon. You will move here, and we will be together. You will work for Air Jamaica. I think I would like a wife who worked for Air Jamaica."

I went along with it, although my detachment was evaporating fast, and I was becoming more frightened by the minute. This guy was delusional! He'd just raped me, threatened me, hurt me—and now he wanted me to marry him? Crazy!

But you're good at dealing with crazy people, I reminded myself. *You do it all the time on planes. Just pretend he's another insane passenger, and you'll be okay.*

When we finally pulled up to the Montego Beach Hotel, Sean and I were chatting easily. He helped me off the moped, then leaned in to kiss me, as if I really was his girlfriend. I tried not to cringe as my lips brushed his.

When I couldn't take it any longer, I pulled away and made a dash for the door, leaving a bewildered Sean staring after me. "Gotta go," I called over my shoulder. "I'll see you later."

He's totally nuts, I thought. I didn't realize at the time that the vision I created as a defense during the rape might have influenced his behavior. Sometimes, people's subconscious minds actually respond to the thoughts we hold about them.

I found Susie in the bar, sharing a cocktail with the other beach boy.

"Where have you been?" she asked. "Are you okay?"

Part of me wanted to tell her everything. But another part of me just wanted to be rid of this day, rid of the fear that was making my body feel cold and numb. The second part won out.

"I'm fine," I said. "Just tired. It's been a long day."

Susie's beach boy looked at me with penetrating dark eyes. I could tell he knew something was up, so I put on a smile and said, "I think I'll take a shower. Those mountain roads are pretty dusty. See you upstairs, Suze."

After locking the door (and checking it twice), I stripped and stepped into the shower. Again and again, I lathered up my body with soap, and let the hot water wash it away. Already, the afternoon seemed like a dream. My body, though sore, was whole, and I found that with a little effort I could turn my thoughts away from the fear.

I'd done a very stupid thing today, going off with Sean—but I'd learned a valuable lesson, too. What I held on to was my choice.

It took hours for the shaking to stop. I visualized myself as a dog shaking off dirty water. None of this was going to cling to me.

I considered going to the authorities. How many other women had Sean violated? How many more would he lure to that secluded beach, if given the opportunity? But I decided against it. I didn't know Sean's last name. Heck, I didn't even know if Sean was his real *first* name. I could never find his mother's shack again; I hadn't been paying attention to the roads we took. And—just like with Captain

B.J.—any charges I made would have been his word against mine. This was 1969, long before the days of rape kits and semen samples. I pictured days of questioning, hours of courtroom drama, my bikini held up as evidence. I didn't want any of it. All I wanted was to get back to New York.

For the rest of our vacation, I stayed by the pool, safe under the watchful eyes of the other guests and the hotel staff. Sean didn't come back around, thank God, and with every hour I spent basking in the sun, the trauma of my experience receded a little more. At times, my mind clawed at me, wanting to clutch and hold the awful story—*I was raped. I was raped! I was raped!*—but I told myself firmly to let it go. By the time Susie and I got on our return flight to JFK, I was pretty much back to my old self.

The only fear which lingered was that Sean had infected me with some awful disease. AIDS hadn't been discovered back then, but there was still syphilis and the clap and a dozen other scary infections to worry about. And what if he'd gotten me pregnant? That thought was nearly as frightening to me as the diseases. A baby could cost me my job: there was no place for a pregnant Stew on United's flight decks. The moment I got back to my apartment, I called my Park Avenue gynecologist and made an emergency appointment.

After the test results came back (negative on all counts, thankfully), I felt that I could truly let the whole experience slide into the past. It had been horrible at the time, but I didn't have to let it continue to affect me. I wasn't going to waste time being afraid. There was too much I wanted to do.

I never told anyone about what happened with Sean—not even Susie. I just didn't feel like dredging it up. And while I exercised necessary caution around unfamiliar people and places from then on, I didn't stop being adventurous.

When you're a metaphysical person, you realize that reacting to challenging life situations is like throwing gasoline on a fire—a fire that can burn you as easily as it does anyone else. I'm not saying that action isn't appropriate—but it should be *considered action*, in alignment with the result you want to create. That way, every step you take comes from a place of integrity and fourth-dimensional consciousness, rather than fear, anger, or baggage. Once you master the art of non-reaction, you can turn almost any situation around. Even rape.

I flew a couple of times with a flight attendant who'd lost her leg in a motorcycle accident. When I first heard about the accident, I would never have expected to find her back in the sky in just a few short months—but suddenly, there she was, a few scars richer but otherwise as full of joy and smiles as she had been before. She had a prosthesis with a mechanical knee that moved almost like a real leg. Three months after her amputation, she was already playing tennis. She wasn't going to give up her life or her career over a lost limb. Rather than attaching to the trauma, she took the lessons she needed from the accident and moved on.

"I'm still me," she was fond of saying. "I just look a little different."

The Biggest Lesson

It has been asserted that the greatest lesson facing any human being on Earth is *forgiveness*. In order to achieve true happiness, divine connection, and liberation, we need to forgive everything and everyone, including ourselves. This concept has been expressed in numerous traditions including Christianity, Kabbalah, Buddhism, and the Hawaiian tradition of Ho'oponopono. Blame is not a creative energy, but a destructive one.

As Colin Tipping writes in *Radical Forgiveness: Making Room for the Miracle:* When you learn to forgive others for everything, you will ultimately reach a place where there is nothing to forgive. While he hung, dying, on the cross, Jesus said, "Father, forgive them, for they know not what they do." If someone shows up in your life and does something terrible, chances are they don't realize (or can't allow themselves to realize) what they're doing. If they had that awareness, they wouldn't act that way.

The reverse is also true. When you refuse to forgive, you're really persecuting yourself. When you're dragging around pain, anger, or sadness because of something someone "did to you," *you* are the one who is suffering. Those negative feelings are projected into the Fourth Dimension—and as we know, the thoughts we project return to us as our reality. After a while, you can become a slave to your own negativity. Negative thoughts block your ability to manifest in a positive manner, because they block your access to G.O.D., which loves all and forgives all. How can you heal if you wish harm on someone else?

When you begin to release your baggage, chances are you'll have to practice forgiveness in the process. Remember that when you forgive someone, you're not letting them off the hook for whatever actions they took. It was never your responsibility to punish them or hold them accountable in the first place. Forgiveness simply frees you from the negative thoughts and patterns you allowed that person's actions toward you to create. By forgiving, you're taking responsibility for your own actions and lessons, and letting the object of your forgiveness take responsibility for theirs.

This sounds wonderful, but it's far easier in theory than in practice, especially if you were raised in what I like to think of as "the old order." Many of us need to bear a cross to feel spiritually secure. This isn't helpful. Jesus's teachings weren't inspired by his death on a cross. They came from a place of love and wholeness, and were delivered almost entirely before his persecution. The crucifixion wasn't some holy rite, but rather the reaction of angry men to a point of view they didn't want to hear. It wasn't his suffering on the cross which made Jesus's sacrifice worthy of remembrance, but the fact that he forgave his tormenters.

In other words, un-awakened people sometimes do cruel and awful things to other people. We can remember the cruelty, and hold up our suffering as a mark of holiness or self-identity—or we can forgive those who harm us, and move on, enlightened, leaving our bricks by the roadside.

What we sow, we reap. In this life or the next, our souls keep coming back to the classroom to learn karmic lessons. There have been a few times—like during my vision of Mother Teresa—when I felt as though I was lifted into my soul. I was neither female nor male, because form is really nothing. There was only an enduring sense of compassion for the little physical me sitting here on Earth. I sensed that this big, soul Me was so powerful and strong that it could take care of any challenge that the weaker, less significant me might encounter—as long as I continued to trust.

I may not have chosen to prosecute either of the men who raped me, but I know that, in one way or another, their negative actions came back to haunt them.

A few years after my graduation from Stew school, Captain B.J. turned up in the first-class cabin on a flight I was working, along with his tired-looking wife. He recognized me, of course, but tried to make it seem as though we were just casual acquaintances. I watched him squirm, his gaze darting between me and his unsuspecting wife. I knew he was waiting for me to blow the whistle on him. His face got so red that I actually wondered if he was having a heart attack.

I could have made a scene. I could have lashed out to "punish" him, but his terror was punishment enough.

I didn't have to live with what he'd done—but he did.

CHAPTER FIVE

The Bunny Club

"You don't have a soul. You are

a Soul; you have a body."

~ CS Lewis

What did I want out of my life in the sky? If you'd asked me in my twenties, I would have said "the good life." I wanted the excitement of exotic destinations, new cultures, and fascinating people. I was living in Greenwich Village, spending weekends in new and exciting locales, strutting like a starlet in my fur coat and heels. Then, operating on the premise of "more is always better," I decided to take my penchant for glamour up a notch. I applied for a job as a Bunny at the Playboy Club.

Despite all that had happened to me out in the wide world, I was still, at this time, more than a little innocent, and I truly believed that this would be a good job for me. After all, I had the body and the personality to pull it off. Unlike the other "gentleman's clubs" of the time, the Playboy Club was considered upscale, classy, and safe. If I got hired as a Bunny, I could double or triple my airline salary. Plus, I'd get to meet a lot of interesting, influential men while wearing what amounted to the sexiest costume in creation.

Looking back now, it's easy to see how immersed I was in the male-dominated culture of the time—but at that point, things just were what they were. I liked being a woman, and I liked being treated like a woman by men. I wasn't a revolutionary, unless you counted my quest for independence and my aversion to marriage. Even by the time 1970 rolled around, women had made relatively few inroads into the boardrooms and corner offices of the world; if you wanted to be independent—and you weren't quite brave enough to be a Gloria Steinem or a Barbara Walters—you found a job where you could put your looks and personality to use. (Interestingly, both of these ladies actually worked as Bunnies for a short time while on assignment. Barbara Walters even did the Bunny Dip on national television!)

At any rate, I was determined to be a part of the glamorous, romantic world of the Bunnies. So I stepped into a smart little skirt, put on my false eyelashes, and took a taxi to the Playboy Club.

After announcing my intention to apply for a job, I was directed to the top floor of the building, where I was met by the "Bunny Mother," a fiercely attractive woman in her forties. Rather than sit me down with an application, she ushered me immediately to a dressing room, where an assistant stripped me of my carefully-chosen outfit. I was given a Bunny costume, which consisted of dark stockings, a pale yellow satin corset, stiletto heels, and a headband with perky bunny ears. The stockings were old and laddered (presumably for having been tried on by dozens of applicants before me). The corset was so tight I could barely breathe; there was no way I could have gotten the zipper up on my own. The metal inserts in the bodice dug painfully into my ribs. Trying not to breathe too deeply, I stepped cautiously into my heels, and the assistant placed the bunny ears on my head.

"Take a look," she said.

I turned to the mirror, and my jaw dropped. "Oh my God! Is that me?"

I barely recognized myself. My waist, pulled in so severely by the corset, was tiny enough to belong to a Barbie doll—while my bust, padded with pantyhose to fill out the leotard, ballooned out like a wasp's behind. My legs looked longer than I'd ever seen them, and the little ears peeking out my coiffed hair… Well, they were even cuter than I'd imagined.

I strutted out of that dressing room feeling like a million bucks.

As I sashayed back to the Bunny Mother's office, a man popped out of one of the doorways. "I'm the club manager," he told me. The way he looked at me told me a little more than that. I stood up straighter—not that I could have slouched in that corset if I'd wanted to.

He walked me back to the office, then disappeared inside. The Bunny Mother said something I couldn't hear, but the manager's reply came through loud and clear. "Hire her," he said.

The door popped open, and he nodded me inside. I entered with a beaming smile on my face. I was going to be a Bunny!

The Bunny Mother had a few questions for me, mostly to do with previous employment. When I told her I was a stewardess, she regarded me thoughtfully. "You know you'll have to give that up eventually. When you're a Bunny, that's all you can be. There's no room for anything else."

The first sliver of doubt began to work its way into my mind. I loved flying, and hadn't imagined that I might have to give it up. Could Bunnyhood possibly be glamorous enough to make up for the loss of my wings?

As those thoughts stewed in my brain, the club photographer slipped into the office. "Congratulations," he said to me. "I'm here to explain how this whole thing works."

The Bunny Mother nodded. "I'll leave you to it."

Turns out, a Bunny's job didn't just involve serving drinks and schmoozing with gentlemen in the club. We were also "encouraged" to pose in various stages of undress for *Playboy* magazine and the club's promotional materials. I would be paid a certain amount of money to pose in my costume, more if I posed half *out* of my costume. Half nude and fully nude would net me even bigger paychecks. If I got chosen as a centerfold, I could receive the equivalent of five years of airline salary for a single photograph.

The glamour-girl part of me loved the thought of all that cash, but my soul was starting to shrivel. It was one thing to use my looks to win over airline passengers and rich club-goers, but quite another to get naked in front of the entire nation. I imagined randy boys all over my hometown pasting my picture up in their barns, and shivered.

But the money... The money was like a hypnotist's pendulum, lulling me into complacency while my dignity was stolen right out from under me.

The photographer left. I sat in a state of near-shock with my bunny tail squashed underneath me and my ears sliding down onto my forehead. I felt like a kid who has just discovered that the Tooth Fairy is really their ordinary, un-magical parent.

The Bunny Mother came back brandishing a thick booklet. "Here's the Bunny manual," she said, handing it to me. "You'll need to come back for training before you start work."

I flipped through the manual, feeling more despondent by the minute. How could there be so many rules? There were rules regarding tail fluffiness, the proper way to do the "Bunny Dip" while carrying a tray, what you could and couldn't eat while working, how to smoke your cigarettes... There were more rules for being a Bunny than there were for being a stewardess!

Still, I resolved not to make a decision right away. This was a job that women all over the country coveted. Even my family thought it was a good idea (probably because they didn't know the bit about the naked pictures). I could make a lot more money than I was making now, and meet the glamorous people I'd always wanted to associate with. Despite the drawbacks, I wondered: could this be a better life than flying?

I left the Bunny Mother's office with a promise that I would come back the following Monday.

That weekend, I flew a trip to Seattle. During my layover, I tossed and turned in my hotel bed. I dreamed that I was a Bunny, working in the New York club. Men in business suits crowded around me as I performed a flawless Bunny Dip. Then, I felt a sharp pull. Suddenly, everyone was clawing at me, trying to yank off my fluffy white tail. I screamed and kicked, but they wouldn't stop.

I jerked awake. The covers were tangled up around my legs. To me, the dream was an irrefutable sign: being a Playboy Bunny was a bad idea.

Later, when I began to truly accept that we are more than our bodies, I understood why my subconscious self had had such an aversion to Bunnyhood. In order to subscribe to the mentality that turned the wheels of the Playboy Club, I would have had to become totally body-identified. My body—how it looked, how it moved, how it did the Bunny Dip—would have become the major definition of *me*.

Women's Lib has gone through many transformations over the years, but some things haven't changed. In fact, I think that more people are body-identified now than they were in the '60s. We—men and women—obsess over how our bodies look, how they feel, what size they are, and how they compare to other bodies. But really, the body is just another component of our physical stuff, a reflection of our consciousness. We create our bodies; they're not an accident. The imperfections we obsess over are just more bricks that keep us from experiencing oneness with G.O.D. and our fourth-dimensional selves. They have no bearing on who we truly are.

We all get the kind of body we need for whatever we're here to experience. The body is a vehicle for the soul in this dimension—no more, no less. Of course, we need to care for our bodies, nourish them, and keep them fit, as pain and discomfort are never helpful. But to put the body foremost in our consciousness is counterproductive; I mean, would you let your "spacesuit" run your life? It's upside-down thinking.

True beauty is the result of harmony, not good bone structure. Disease in the body is often a result of unhealthy thoughts in the mind. Since the body is a reflection of thought, it follows that harmonious thoughts create health and ease, while disharmonious thoughts create dis-ease. Stress and anxiety constrict the whole body, making it hard to find an open channel to the fourth-dimensional self. But once the mind is in alignment with G.O.D., anything can be healed. No matter how much time you spend rolling in the mud, you can always find a way to get clean. You simply have to be willing to do some housekeeping.

Our bodies are primal, tied to this plane of existence; our physical desire to mate and procreate is very real. This is not the same as the desire of the soul (the fourth-dimensional Self) to experience love—however, the human mind likes to entangle these two desires until they feel inseparable. We believe that being beautiful and desirable will bring us love, so we chase after human beauty with plastic surgery, pills, clothes, and cosmetics. But real love is part of G.O.D., and divine; it's a connection of souls, not bodies, and it can't be found through mundane means.

When you learn to separate love from human sexuality, you'll unload a lot of bricks, I promise.

I didn't go back to the Bunny Club that Monday. And while I visited a few times over the years with male friends, I never again desired to shove myself into that corset.

Years after my encounter with the Bunny Mother, while visiting my hometown, I ran into some high school friends at the local bar. Thanks to some big mouths, everyone in town knew that I'd been offered a job as a Bunny, and the boys were always on the lookout for photos of me.

As I sipped my drink, one guy swaggered up to me. Leaning very close, he whispered, "I saw you in *Playboy*." The awe in his tone was such that he might have been saying, "I saw you on that spaceship."

"Sorry, I wasn't in *Playboy*," I told him firmly.

"Come on! You're a Bunny. Everyone heard about it! And I *know* it was your ass in that picture."

"I'm telling you, it wasn't me!" But inside, I started to giggle. This was just more confirmation that I'd made the right choice. Had I gone that route, I would have eventually been reduced to nothing more than, well, an ass.

Looking Beyond the Mirror

Our bodies are temporary. Every cell in their amazingly complex structure is replaced every seven or so years. That means that even if you look almost the same on the outside, you are not the same person you were a year ago. You're a *completely* different person physically than you were seven years ago, because not a single solitary cell of that seven-years-ago self remains! And yet, who you really are stays the same.

We experience longer arcs of change as well. While our human bodies age and eventually die, our fourth-dimensional selves—our souls—remain whole. When the work we chose to undertake in this world is accomplished, the body is surrendered. As fourth-dimensional beings, we may wear many bodies—in, some teachers say, many dimensions beyond the one which we are currently experiencing.

Even after I said no to the Bunny tail, I remained fairly body-identified throughout my twenties. I knew that I was beautiful, and that I could use my beauty to get ahead in the world. But while I wore my face and body as if it was the only one that had ever belonged to me, I knew deep down that my soul was far older than my two-and-a-half decades.

This was proven to me by my friend Earl, a Tarot reader and metaphysical teacher who lived in New York. On one pitch-black, moonless night, he set up a mirror in my apartment. It was an old-fashioned mirror, the kind with quicksilver on the back. He placed candles on either side, about six inches in front of the glass, turned out all the lights, and drew the curtains across the windows.

"Stare into your own eyes in the mirror," he told me. "Go into daydream."

Always up for an adventure, I situated myself on a chair, and did as he instructed. "What will I see?" I asked.

"Who you were before you came here. Your past lives." His voice was smoky, as if I was hearing it on the wind from a long way away.

Fascinated, I gazed into my own eyes. The candle flame was reflected in my irises; it turned them golden. The face around my eyes started to blur.

A few heartbeats later, I found myself looking at a Native American man with long, wavy hair and a hawkish nose. He was so serene and beautiful, I wanted to reach out to him—but then the face changed again. I saw a round-faced, olive-skinned Italian matron with dark hair pulled severely away from her face, like a woman in a Renaissance painting.

The images started to scroll faster. I saw a rough-hewn frontiersman, a dainty Victorian female, an androgynous face shadowed by a dark hood. There were many more, coming and going so quickly that I could barely see them. But all of them had the same eyes—*my* eyes. I had been all of these people, and all of these people were inside of me!

"Did you see them?" I asked Earl breathlessly as I came out of my trance. "Did you see who I was?"

"I did. You carry a lot of wisdom, Rebecca. You just have to remember that you have it."

That day, I set aside a lot of the physical baggage I was carrying. My body was a wonderful thing—but it wasn't *me,* any more than all of those other bodies and faces had been me. The *true* me was the constant, bright soul looking out from those unchanging eyes.

Spiritual Surgery

Our reactions to encounters with our baggage and the baggage of others create secondary reactions in our bodies. You've doubtless heard that ninety-nine percent of disease is a direct result of stress? Well, stress is a direct result of your encounters with your internal bricks. Stress shows you where you are no longer in alignment with the divine principles of love, health, abundance, joy, oneness, and reciprocity.

Majorly stressful situations like divorce, the death of a loved one, the desertion of a friend or child, or a major financial upset force us to evaluate, accept, and (hopefully) set aside many of our bricks at once. The process of self-evolution isn't necessarily stressful, although it can be challenging. The real stress shows up when we *resist* this process—and stress, in turn, creates disease.

Numerous studies by the medical community have analyzed the connection between stressful life situations and major illnesses. Obviously, cardiac disease is linked to stress. How often have you said to someone, "Calm down, before you give yourself a heart attack!" Links have also been established between divorce and breast cancer, and between general emotional stress and prostate cancer. The Greek physician Claudius Galen, in *De Tumoribus*, his treatise on tumors, observed that "melancholy" women were much more likely to develop cancerous tumors than happy women. In 1701, the English physician Gendron noted that cancer seemed to be linked to "disasters of life as occasion much trouble and grief." Researchers today are coming to the same conclusions: when our minds are troubled, our bodies are troubled.

All my young life, cancer was my greatest fear. I could barely speak the word. But what we think about, we attract. I'm certain that I developed cervical cancer as a result of that fear—and of the emotional turbulence generated by my affair with a married man.

In my mid-twenties, I decided it was time to get out of New York. The constant buzz of the city was starting to get to me. Greenwich Village no longer felt like a restful place to call home. So I applied for a transfer to the West Coast, and found myself a beautiful apartment in Belvedere, California with an ocean view and two fun-loving Stew roommates.

At first, I didn't know Robert was married. (In case you're wondering, yes, this is the same Robert who introduced me to his Japanese friend as a television personality.) We met in the air on a cross-country flight. He was dashing, a romantic older man who really knew how to make a girl feel special. Whenever I was on the ground, he would take me out and spoil me. I chose my flight schedule so we could meet on his business trips in fascinating, worldly locations.

We didn't talk about marriage. After all, I didn't want to be married; I was too happy globe-trotting in my sassy Stew uniform. But it never occurred to me that I was a mistress until six months after we started dating, when Robert and I traveled together to Mexico City. While taking a bath, I overheard him making a phone call in the other room. Back then, you had to go through the hotel operator to place a call, and I recognized the California area code. Curious, I wrote the number in eyeliner pencil on a scrap of toilet paper and tucked it away.

Not long after we got home, Robert asked me to meet him at Coit Tower in San Francisco. It was like a movie, with the repentant hero confessing to his lover that he was a liar and a cheat. All we needed was a sappy soundtrack.

"I want to be with you," he told me in his most piteous voice. "I'll get a divorce. You just have to give me some time!"

That night, I called the number I'd overheard him giving the operator in Mexico. A sweet-voiced girl answered. When I asked for Robert, she held the phone away from her ear and called, "Daddy! There's a woman on the phone for you!"

Somehow, Robert had forgotten to include the small fact of fatherhood in his over-dramatized confession.

I didn't want to waste my time going out with a married man, but he promised that he'd divorce his wife if I could just give him some time, and I believed him. I mean, he seemed to be nuts about me. I felt a little guilty, but consoled myself with the thought that all the wrongdoing was on his end. *I* wasn't the one cheating. Maybe, I reasoned, this wife of his even deserved to be cheated on.

So I waited... and waited.

By the time I was twenty-seven, I'd been with Robert for almost four years, and was carrying a lot of unease and frustration about the relationship. It was almost like it was short-circuiting me. I knew he was leading a double life, but I couldn't seem to break away. To me, he was the ultimate ideal of high romance—and I was a sucker for romance.

That autumn, I went to the doctor for a routine checkup and PAP smear. A few days later, the doctor called me at home. His voice was full of concern. "I'd like you to come back for a second exam next week. Your test revealed some abnormalities."

That second exam led to a biopsy. Three days after that, the phone rang again.

"Go straight to the hospital and get scheduled for surgery," my doctor said. "You have cervical cancer, and we want to perform a hysterectomy."

"Surgery?" I whispered. "Are you sure?"

"If you don't have this surgery, you'll be dead by the time you're forty."

By that point in my young life, I'd survived awful turbulence, mid-air near-misses, rape, and two car accidents. But I've never known such fear, before or since, as I knew that day in my kitchen in Belvedere. My worst nightmares had come true. There was something growing inside me that was going to kill me. I wanted to climb out of my skin.

To let someone cut open my body and remove an organ I was born with was unacceptable to me—but according to my doctor, I had only two options: death or mutilation.

There had to be another solution.

We live in a universe where mind is greater than matter; a place where transformation of thought can equal transformation of circumstance. Nothing is good or bad, not even death. Everything just *is*. This is the truth offered by metaphysics. When things are at their most dire, when there's nowhere left to turn in the material world and no human solution to the problem, we are forced to become infinitely more creative. This creativity in the midst of turbulence can spark our most transformative experiences.

People find G.O.D. in one of two ways: through fear, or through love. For most, fear is the pathway. When you're in a state of profound fear—as I was—there's the potential for a breakthrough to occur: an "Ah-ha!" moment. There's simply nowhere else for the mind to go.

Trembling with fear, telephone dangling from my hand, I opened myself to the possibility that there might be another answer for me. And the answer appeared.

Just before my diagnosis, I'd met a man who'd been healed of a brain tumor through Christian Science. After speaking with him, I attended a service at the local branch church, but I still didn't really know anything about Mary Baker Eddy and her teachings. What I *did* know was that if spiritual healing had worked for my friend, there was no reason why it couldn't work for me, too. I picked up a copy of the Christian Science Journal and made an appointment with a local practitioner.

As I drove to the practitioner's house, I felt completely loaded down with fear. The weight of it was unbearable. I had no idea what this healing would entail. Would there be laying on of hands, like in the Bible? Would I have to undress? Would it be invasive, or creepy?

But the healing entailed none of these things. The practitioner sat me down in a comfortable chair and began to speak in a kind, loving voice. She said I was a perfect child of God, and that perfect health was my birthright. As she spoke, the weight of my terror lifted, and a beautiful presence enfolded my whole body. I believed every word she said because I could feel G.O.D.'s loving presence all around me. As long as I trusted in divine goodness and omnipotence, I would always be whole, safe, and healthy.

I walked out of that practitioner's office a changed person. The experience had been totally mind-blowing and, at the same time, perfectly natural. All the fear, anxiety, and depression I'd been fighting for years just... evaporated. My body had changed—but more importantly, my mind and soul had changed. Nothing about my life would ever be the same.

I never called my doctor to tell him I was healed. I didn't feel any need to revisit a situation that was behind me. However, a year later, a doctor on the East Coast performed a separate examination and found only healthy tissue. It was as if my cancer had never been.

The physical healing, however dramatic, was the least of the benefits I received from that Christian Science treatment. I felt like my brain was full of iron filings, and a magnet had been held over them, making them all stand on end. Any time I prayed or meditated, I could feel the grace of G.O.D. flowing through my body like I was standing in a spiritual waterfall. For a year, I didn't see a drop of rain. Wherever I traveled, the sun shone brilliantly over my head. Beauty was everywhere: I saw the hand of Grace in the flowers, people, dogs, and trees. All were stunning and divine; all were part of G.O.D. and creation.

One day, while contemplating this sparkling new world, I came to a profound realization: *there is only one God.* I thought I already knew that—but as it turned out, I didn't. Every name for God, every definition, is a product of the material dimension. How can we put a single name to that which is everything? And what's more, how can we love God by one name and hate Him by another?

If God was everywhere and in everything, and there was only one God, then God was in me, and I was in God! All of the power and energy of the Universe was at my fingertips, and I could create anything I wanted simply by thinking about it. The truth of my oneness was incredibly powerful, and yet so easy to overlook that I'd missed it for years.

On the heels of that revelation, more knots were untied in my consciousness. Thoughts and behaviors I had accepted as natural felt suddenly wrong, and I realized that I'd been kidding myself in a lot of areas of my life. Beliefs I had once accepted without question started to erode. I realized that I'd only been putting Band-Aids on my problems, not solving them—and the result had been unease in my mind and disease in my body.

The more ways I found to live closer to my true nature, the more pronounced these changes became. All my filters were wiped clean. Without my old habits and The Rules to cloud my perception, I began to observe that people I'd once thought wise and worldly suffered from the same limited thinking from which I had just been freed. They were going through the motions of their lives like marionettes, never knowing that they held their own strings.

The day after my healing, my roommate Kitty and I decided to head into San Francisco to visit a popular bar. I was in a state of bliss, so I didn't really care what we did, but she wanted to be seen in one particular place for happy hour. As we got our drinks, a friend of Kitty's sidled up to us. He was a hotshot young lawyer on the fast track to millionaire status—and Kitty was the ultimate material girl, willing to do anything to get a guy with big bucks. In a span of seconds, her whole demeanor shifted.

I sat on my bar stool in awe as the courtship (or maybe "hunt" would be the better word) unfolded between Kitty and the lawyer. It was like watching two puppets. They were playing the ultimate human game, tossing out words and gestures calculated to create a reaction. There was no substance behind anything they were saying; each phrase was a blatant attempt to create the response each wanted from the other. It made me feel ill.

Thirty minutes in, I couldn't take it anymore. Leaving Kitty to find her own way home, I fled back to Marin County.

Hoping to find someone with whom I could connect in a reasonable way, I dropped by the apartment of an English friend in Sausalito—only to find him in the heat of that same human game with his on-again, off-again girlfriend. He wanted her to be a certain way, she wanted him to change. I could see their desire for each other clearly, but they couldn't see that desire in one another through the clouds of doubt and anger that surrounded them.

I had to get out of that situation, too. Wrapped up in their drama, they didn't even see me leave.

Apparently, whatever had shifted in me was making it very difficult to relate to people in the way I was used to. People I'd considered close friends weren't who I thought they were. They weren't authentic; they were barely aware. How had I not seen this before?

Had *I* been doing these same things, playing the same games?

The answer was obvious. Of course I had! I'd been dating a married man for four years. I let him pull my strings, and told myself that he alone had the power to fulfill me. But now, I knew the truth: I was the only one who could sustain me, because I was one with G.O.D.

The extreme clarity that set in while I was in the bar with Kitty lasted only three days; things started to soften after that. In fact, by the time my next luncheon date with Robert came around, I was actually looking forward to seeing him and sharing my miraculous transformation. Despite his materialism and obvious character flaws, he was an avid student of metaphysics—particularly of Gurdjieff, to whose work he'd introduced me a few years before—and I knew he'd be fascinated by my spiritual healing experience.

When he walked in the door, I felt... nothing. None of the usual butterflies in my stomach, none of the old romance. Instead, I saw a man fifteen years my senior, bowed by the weight of his lies, filled with fear that those lies might unravel.

I realized, as I watched him walk across the restaurant (conscious, as always, of every pretty woman's eyes on him), that I had been in love with an illusion. I had made Robert a false god, giving him authority over my happiness; I had worshipped him as the embodiment of my romantic vision.

Now, I had stepped out of the game. I was more interested in finding out what was real, and exploring my relationship not to other human beings, but to this divine energy which filled me to the brim. My relationship with Robert had run its course. He was never going to leave his wife, and I was no longer content to hover in the limbo of an adulterous relationship.

"I'm here to say goodbye," I told him.

He didn't seem upset, or even surprised. He listened to the story of my healing with real curiosity and agreed that I'd been given a profound gift, an understanding that he himself had been seeking for years.

"You've changed," he said, as we were getting ready to leave. "I think you're going to be a healer one day."

I smiled. "Maybe I will."

Are You In There?

The Australian Aboriginal peoples have a tradition: when they meet, they look deep into one another's eyes, and ask, "Are you in there?" To which the other replies, "I'm here." It's a call to the true Self to emerge and be known. I started trying this out on my girlfriends and a number of handsome bachelors in Marin County. I would stare into someone's eyes until there was a shift. Suddenly, I'd know I was seeing their pure essence. When the façade dropped, inevitably the person would freak out. It was like I had stripped them totally naked.

"What are you doing?" they'd cry. "I can't handle it!"

I began to see that everyone I knew was hiding behind something: ego, money, ambition, worldly accomplishments. But what they showed the world was entirely different than what they felt inside.

I started healing my flying partners in mid-air. When someone was coming down with a cold, I would look deep into his or her eyes and say, "You are perfectly healthy. There is nothing wrong with you." Soon, their symptoms would disappear because they believed that I had the power to heal them—and because I believed that they, like me, held the power of G.O.D. inside them.

I also found that I could be completely, unabashedly myself in every situation. I'd always been outgoing, but after my healing I no longer worried what anyone thought of me. I had no more hang-ups.

After a while, the intensity of my connection to the Fourth Dimension grew gentler. I no longer felt like I had magnets in my head, but I knew that that attuned state was there waiting for me whenever I chose to visit it. I suppose masters like Jesus and Buddha were in that state all the time—always able to access their divinity and see the latent beauty in people—but for a regular person like me, it was truly a gift to be able to experience that kind of intensity.

As I delved deeper, my desire to get out of California grew stronger. I needed to break the spell of the lifestyle I'd been living, and the people I'd been living it with. Wherever I went, I couldn't escape that vision of my friends as puppets. Also, I wanted to find out more about my healing and meet people who could relate to what

I'd experienced. So I headed back to my hometown of Westport to regroup and figure out my next move.

I don't know what I was expecting from my family and friends back East—but I soon became very, very aware that I was the only person in my sphere operating at this frequency. I told my parents about my healing. They didn't believe me. "I've never heard of such a thing," my mother said. I had a cousin who was a Christian Scientist; everyone passed her off as an eccentric, and I quickly attained the same questionable status.

The positive side of this experience was that no matter what rocks my family and friends threw at me, they just bounced off. Unlike with my friends on the West Coast, I was able to be non-reactive. I still couldn't understand why my family (or anyone) would turn their back on evidence of true spiritual healing, but I was able to accept their choice.

A few months after my cross-country move, I had another revelation. My cancer had been caused not by some physical abnormality or deficiency, but by the energetic fallout of my affair with Robert. He hadn't been the only guilty party in the relationship. He was an adulterer, but *I was an adulteress.* I could no longer deny it. By carrying on a four-year affair with a married man, I had betrayed Robert's wife—a woman I'd never met, but harbored all kinds of nasty thoughts about nonetheless—his young daughter, and my own ideals of love. By harming myself, I had harmed them, and by harming them, I had also harmed myself. We were all connected in the intricate web of the Universe.

I have no idea what happened to Robert after I left California. I'm sure he moved on to another mistress, and I'm sure she fell for him as hard as I did. I could only hope that whoever took my place learned at least a few of the intense, painful, and beautiful lessons that I learned as a result of that experience.

CHAPTER SIX

Great Expectations

> *"You create your own universe as you go along."*
> ~ *Winston Churchill*

The great teachers say that you attract the people you are supposed to be working with, playing with, hanging out with, or teaching, because the vibratory frequency of your thought will draw them to you.

Our reality is always a projection of our thought. We draw into our experience the things which we value. People who obsess about their looks tend to attract others who do the same. People who value intellect tend to attract other intellectuals. When our values change, the people around us either shift into alignment with our new vibration, or move away to find a vibration that serves their own purpose more fully.

As a young twenty-something I decided that, if I ever had to stop flying, I wanted to own a modeling agency. I had a grand vision of all the beautiful people conspiring to take beautiful pictures for beautiful magazines, or to walk beautifully down the runways in beautiful designer clothes. I wanted to be part of that beauty so badly that I literally programmed it into my mind.

After my spiritual healing, those aspirations were blurred. In those first few days after my treatment, I got a clear glimpse of what human programing really looked like. Beauty, I saw, had little to do with our human bodies, and everything to do with divine alignment. But then, the clarity softened. Over the next three years, I backslid toward my old ways of thinking, and my fascination with beauty once again reared its perfectly coiffed head.

When I turned thirty, I decided I wanted to get married.

I had no idea whom I was going to marry. I wasn't even dating anyone. But something inside me said my time had come.

A short few months later, I met Jeremy Lynch on a coast-to-coast flight.

If the name sounds familiar, I'm not surprised. Jeremy was a hugely successful male model in the 1970s. He was the Winston Man, six and a half feet tall, larger than life, the iconic face of a dozen designers. He was *gorgeous*. He was also funny, engaging, well-read, and well-travelled.

"You have such lovely eyes," he told me, as I batted my false eyelashes at him.

I won't lie. I was in love pretty much from the start.

We did the cross-continental dating thing for a while before making the big move. After my brief stint in Westport post-Robert, I'd moved back to California. Jeremy was based in New York. When it was clear that we were getting serious, I put in for yet another transfer and moved into Jeremy's loft near the Fashion Institute in Manhattan.

We were married on Valentine's Day, 1977. I woke up that day with a knot in the pit of my stomach; apparently, I hadn't completely gotten over my aversion to marriage. But

Jeremy insisted, and I went along despite my reservations. After all, this was what I'd wanted, right?

We exchanged our vows at City Hall, in front of a judge and one witness (an actor friend of Jeremy's). Jeremy didn't want a big, public wedding; he liked to be perceived as single yet unattainable. It was all part of his public persona.

My beauty-related programming was fulfilled not long afterward, when Jeremy and I co-founded Jeremy Lynch Models, Inc. Over the next three years, I learned a lot about how the modeling, movie, and television industries operate. The magic of it all was stripped away—and although what was revealed was fascinating in its own right, none of it was as glamorous as I'd first believed.

As human beings, we have a *thing* about beauty. We worship it; we give our thought and energy to it. Even when we hate or envy it, we love it. Why? I'm not sure. Maybe it's because we're always looking to catch a glimpse of divine beauty on this three-dimensional plane. Maybe it's because our human minds are programmed to discern symmetry and pleasing shapes. Maybe it's just because The Rules say we should.

Whatever the reason, beautiful people are treated differently than "normal" people. We say things like, "He has it made!" or, "Look at her: what on earth could *she* have to worry about?" Even as we worship at the altar of physical beauty, we hold those who possess it to a higher standard, forgetting that we all have baggage to sort out and negative programming to unravel.

In the modeling industry, there are those who have what we used to call "severe beauty," an almost otherworldly quality that makes people stop and stare at them on the street, or react to them in odd ways. Even I was taken aback by some of the faces and bodies that strutted through our offices. But I quickly realized that there is a flip side to everything. Some of these exceptional-looking people were severely underdeveloped in other areas. They were used to getting their own way, and threw tantrums when they didn't. They had become so used to people doing things for them that they couldn't even run their own lives. They didn't need career management; they needed babysitting.

As time went on, I began to see these same tendencies in Jeremy. Everywhere we went, we got better service, better seats, better prices. We got complimentary limo rides and VIP access to all the best clubs. All he had to do was flash his modeling card, and people would fall over themselves to serve him, hoping for a glimpse of that megawatt smile.

When I first moved into Jeremy's loft, every available wall surface was papered with his posters and headshots. I had quite a battle to get him to take even a few of them down. Sometimes, he would wake up in the middle of the night, filled with anxiety about some project or other—but instead of watching television or reading, he'd open his modeling portfolio, and flip through the iconic images that spanned his career. "At least I'm gorgeous," he'd say, when he had finally calmed down enough to get back into bed. "I've got that going for me."

When he suggested we put a mirror on the bedroom ceiling, I had to put my foot down.

At first, I thought the whole Narcissus thing was some kind of joke. Was it even possible for a real person to be so self-absorbed? Over time, however, I came to realize that many people need daily validation to cope with their lives. Some are constantly checking their bank balances, soothing their anxiety with the security of a fat savings account. Some identify with their beautiful homes. Some attach themselves to high-profile careers or exclusive social groups. Still others define themselves by their rock-hard abs, their height, their weight, their rebellious behaviors, their eclectic style of dress... I could go on, but why bother? All these things are transient. In terms of who we really are, they mean nothing.

For me, it was interesting to live with someone so body-identified, and to be part of a business that made its money off of physical beauty. It made me conscious of how much I identified myself as a sexy Stew, a worldly traveler, a free spirit. I had always sought out beauty and glamour in the air—but on the ground with my husband, I found myself shying away, remembering the plethora of faces and lives I'd glimpsed in the mirror with Earl. I delved into my metaphysical books, looking for evidence that we are more than our bodies. And all the while, I spent my days screening potential models, selecting candidates based on the same ephemeral physical loveliness I was striving so hard to see beyond.

People came to us from all over the country. They strutted or slunk or wobbled across the open room where I had my desk, clutching their headshots in nervous hands. "Am I good enough?" they would ask me. As I answered yes or no, I was acutely conscious of the fact that their very lives hung on my words. They had made me a goddess, with the power to fulfill their wildest dreams or shatter their fondest hopes. Every day, at least one young aspirant would sob on my shoulder because her hips were too wide for designer samples, or his cheekbones weren't chiseled enough for print work.

It should come as no surprise that the modeling industry has a high rate of "disintegration." There's too much pressure, too much partying, too much sex, too much desire. Some of the young women on my roster would literally do anything to get jobs—and I mean *anything.* Some of the young men were the same. The more they debased themselves to get work, the more insecure they felt—and the more work they needed to feel good. It was a depressing cycle.

Using their beauty commercially gives some people the ego stroke they need in the moment—but like everything else on this physical plane, beauty is impermanent. It goes away. It gets scratched and dented; it grows old. This might seem obvious to you or me, but that truth can shatter someone whose entire existence is based on bone structure.

Another interesting side of the industry I witnessed came from those who weren't in the industry. There are men out there who would sell their souls to date a model. There were always guys hanging around our office, trying to pick up beautiful young girls so they could claim a lifestyle beyond that of the average jerk. But beauty is no substitute for substance, and fulfillment of desire is not the key to happiness. After a few months of dating one girl, they'd dump her on some flimsy pretext or other, and come back to our offices to hook another one, totally unaware of the real reason for their discontent.

When you're tapped in to the Fourth Dimension and the divine laws, your dreams are never unattainable. But as I discovered, when you're caught in the trap of thinking that beauty has the power to satisfy, you're always running from one beautiful thing to another, looking for material perfection that doesn't exist. As they say, the pursuit of happiness is the source of all unhappiness.

During this time, I found some grounding through my spiritual practices. I regularly attended services at the Christian Science church on Fifth Avenue. I was hungry to deepen my connection to the divine and recapture that "magnetized" feeling I'd experienced after my healing. The more time I spent in the shallow waters of the fashion industry, the more important that connection became.

On the stiflingly hot evening of July 13, 1977, after seeing Jeremy off to the airport for a modeling gig in Berlin, I attended a healing testimony service at the Christian Science church. Despite the stuffy air, I left feeling lighter than I had in weeks. No matter what happened in my life, I felt, I would be taken care of. I had been healed of cancer: after that, nothing else could be that difficult.

As I ate my dinner in a small café on Madison Avenue, the lights went out. All of them, as far as the eye could see. The city that never sleeps was abruptly plunged into total darkness.

The owner (apologizing profusely, although he obviously had nothing to do with the blackout) lit candles for me and the one other couple who were still eating. Flashlights winked in the darkness outside. There was a palpable furtiveness to the action on the street, as if the blackout had turned everyone into a cat burglar. A few passersby poked their heads in to give the owner the update on the conditions in midtown. There was speculation about looting.

The restaurateur shook his head. "People are damned opportunists," he muttered. Then, he turned to me. "What are you going to do, young lady? Will you be able to get home safely?"

"Actually..." I hadn't considered it until now, but our loft was accessible only by the freight elevator that had served the building since it had been a warehouse—and the elevator ran on electricity.

I couldn't go home.

On any other night, I might have been twitching with fear. People were running wild in the dark, and my husband was three thousand miles away in Germany. But I was still in that spiritual space where nothing could harm me unless I allowed it.

I calmly picked up my fork. "I'll figure something out," I said.

The owner regarded me quizzically, but the couple at the next table turned around. "I couldn't help overhearing," the woman said. "You can stay in our daughter's bedroom if you like. She's out of town."

Whatever people say about New Yorkers, you can always count on them to come through in a tight spot. I went home with the couple to their posh apartment on the East Side. There wasn't much conversation; with no light to see by, we all just went to bed. I slept like a baby, feeling perfectly protected and safe.

By the next morning, the lights were back on. I had an early flight, so I left a thank you note on the counter and tiptoed out the door without waking my hosts. For weeks afterward, I lived in a sense of profound gratitude for the generosity of strangers and the spiritual connectedness that could offer me protection in even the strangest circumstances.

Soon, however, that connectedness faded once again into the reality of daily life with Jeremy. About three months after the blackout, we decided it was time to move out of the loft. I wasn't comfortable there. Something about the energy was off. We would come home to find things moved or missing, with no explanation. I thought maybe we had a ghost. (We later found out that our upstairs neighbor had been coming in through the ceiling to steal from us!)

Plus, we'd acquired a squatter: a young actor friend of Jeremy's named Peter who camped out on our couch between jobs. The guy was a loose cannon, a partier, and a mooch. I wanted him gone, but he just wouldn't leave. Even after all of our furniture had been relocated to our new place on East 81st Street, our unwanted guest refused to budge. Peter had this idea that he and Jeremy were working together, that he was somehow going to be an asset to the agency. Despite Jeremy's repeated attempts at intervention, there was no getting through to him. Peter needed somewhere to live, and our place was his place. Period.

Anger and frustration were building in my body like a bonfire. We were under pressure from the landlord to clear out, but apart from physically removing Peter from the space (and suffering the bruises) there was nothing we could do. By the time I boarded my next cross-country flight, I could practically feel steam coming out of my ears.

Once I landed in California, I drove out to Marin County to visit my brother Daniel and his wife Pam. The trip hadn't gone smoothly; in fact, it seemed like all the passengers were at one another's throats. Usually I could stay above it all, but my own anger was at a boil, and the turmoil on board only fed it.

My brother wasn't home, but he was expecting me, so I let myself in to the house and lay down for a nap. An hour later, I woke in shattering pain.

I'd never felt anything like this before. It was like someone had skewered me with a hot poker through the right side of my belly. I tried to stand, but couldn't straighten up. So I crawled, gasping, out of the bedroom and toward the kitchen, where the phone should have been. I didn't know what was happening, but I needed treatment. Now.

Only, there was no phone. Daniel and his wife had just moved into this house, and the service hadn't been hooked up yet. There was no way I could drive—I couldn't even walk—so I curled up in a shivering ball on the tile and waited for someone to come home.

Pam found me like that a couple of hours later. She went white, as if I'd punched her in the gut—which was kind of how I was feeling at that moment. "We have to get you to the hospital," she said. "I think you're having an appendicitis attack."

I shook my head weakly. "No. They'll want to cut me open. Call a Christian Science practitioner. Please. There should be someone in the phone book."

"Rebecca, I really think—"

"No hospital!"

"Okay, if you say so." Clearly, she thought I was delirious. But she ran across the street to the yacht club and called the first practitioner she found in the phone book.

From my place on the kitchen floor, I felt a shift the moment the call connected. I sensed an orange light all around me, pulsating as I drifted in and out of consciousness. Then, from my left, a voice said, *"Love that man with all your heart."*

Immediately, I knew who I was hating. I held the idea that Peter was messing up my life, preventing me from realizing my goal of moving to our new, more comfortable apartment. I resented his power over me and my circumstances—but in reality, *I* was choosing to give him that power by reacting to him with anger and hatred. Just like me, Peter was a divine being, worthy of my compassion—but he had no more power over my reality than I had over his. Once I acknowledged this, my anger dissolved. Then, there was a shift—a click in my belly, like a gear shifting back into place. The pain was immediately relieved.

Once again, I had experienced an instantaneous spiritual healing.

I was weak for a couple of days, but soon felt well enough to fly. When I got back to New York, I calmly informed Peter that while I was truly sorry for his situation, he needed to leave, or he'd be hearing from our lawyer. There was no drama; I didn't feel like I wanted to attack him anymore. I was truly determined to love this man with all my heart.

Two days and one legal letter later, Peter was gone for good. We got our deposit back from the landlord without a problem. While I didn't quite frame my feelings in terms of "baggage" back then, it was evident to me that when I stopped holding so much intense emotion around the situation, things resolved themselves with a minimum of strife. My own anger had been blocking the divine flow of events, and it had literally made me sick.

After that, I looked more closely at the emotions I held around the people and situations in my life, and found a lot of things that needed to be unpacked—including my feelings about beauty and glamour.

As you can probably imagine, this didn't bode well for my marriage.

Stayin' Alive

When Jeremy wasn't modeling, acting, or helping me manage our agency, he worked as a doorman at Studio 54. Everyone went there, from royalty to movie stars to average Joes and Janes. And *everyone* knew Jeremy.

There was a fascinating subculture around Studio 54. I had friends who would work all day, and stay up dancing and doing cocaine all night. They wouldn't sleep for days, sometimes weeks at a stretch. When I suggested they get some rest before they keeled over, they looked at me like I'd just suggested they shoot their mother. *Anyone* could show up at Studio 54, they told me, and they weren't going to miss a second of the action. Who was to say whom they might dance with, do blow with, hook up with?

I only went to the club a handful of times. I didn't find it all that appealing; I had enough superficiality in my day job. And while I wasn't a prude by any stretch, the amount of sex going on there shocked me. To the regulars, sex was just part of the scene, the natural progression of yet another crazy night out. (It was only years later, when some of the most prominent personalities on the scene started dying of AIDS, that they finally realized they were throwing away their lives for a thrill.)

One woman I knew, Anais, was a regular at Studio 54. She had been abused as a child, and had recently escaped from an abusive German boyfriend overseas. She had outfits that belonged on a Broadway stage, and a boob job that surpassed anything nature could have engineered. Every night, she twirled around the dance floor, hoping her Prince Charming would see her in the glory of the strobe lights, sweep her off her feet, and carry her away to a fairy-tale life as his "Dancing Queen." And every morning, when she woke up in her bed (or someone else's) she was disappointed. What she was really looking for was a stable, loving relationship; what she got were the bitter dregs of the party scene.

The truth that escaped Anais is the same one of which I remind myself daily: *we are not our bodies, and we are not our minds.* We are divine ideas. When we align with that, the rest just falls into place. We don't have to qualify for love through our looks, our possessions, our contacts, or anything else. We don't have to worry about being loved, because we *are* love.

All in all, the world of modeling and fashion wasn't what I'd dreamed it would be. As I became more and more disillusioned with the industry, I also found myself disillusioned with Jeremy. He was truly a product of his environment, and while he was a good person at heart, in the end, I couldn't compete with his image of himself. Nor could I cater to his every whim the way others in his life did. I think he resented that a bit. I was used to being independent; he was used to being adored.

In 1981 we got an offer to manage an Elite modeling agency in Boston. We were still running our own agency, but this was a great opportunity to play with the big boys. Jeremy did some work with Elite; they got him his biggest jobs. "If you take this seriously," they told him, "You could make a fortune."

I was all for it. Working with Elite would mean less involvement for me on a day-to-day basis—but Jeremy wasn't interested. He didn't want to turn over the up-and-comers he'd discovered through Jeremy Lynch Models to anyone else, even his own employing agency. Still, the idea of a new market was enough to lure him to Boston, so we packed up and headed north.

While Boston is a big city in some respects, it's a small town in others, and it has very little of the glitter or pizzazz of New York. Jeremy was totally out of his comfort zone. He wasn't getting the jobs he wanted, or the star treatment he thought he deserved. The people at the hot restaurants and hotel bars had no idea who he was. His modeling card no longer got him the best seat in the house, and he never got ushered to the front of the line at the clubs.

He also hated doing desk work. The result of this was that he expected me to take care of the day-to-day business of the agency—which in the beginning, I had done willingly. However, I was becoming so frustrated by the industry that I wanted less and less to do with the agency myself. I would rather spend my time flying. As you can imagine, this led to some pretty harsh arguments. I was regularly driven to tears when we were out to dinner. The less interested I became in Jeremy as a brand, the less interested he was in me as a wife. Accountability wasn't at all appealing to him. He couldn't bear the thought of someone "expecting" things from him. The more I pulled back, the more volatile he became.

We were both obviously unhappy, but Jeremy wasn't one to take rejection lightly. When I finally told him I was leaving him, he completely flipped out. Looking back, I realize my timing was less than ideal; we were out at a bar with Earl and my brother, and we'd both been drinking. I said my piece in the semi-privacy of the bar's back hallway, thinking that he would be as relieved as I was by the idea of a divorce. Instead, Jeremy pushed me aside and stormed out, leaving me gasping outside the bathrooms.

I made to follow him, but Earl grabbed my elbow. "Let him cool off," he told me. "You know you can't talk to him when he's like this."

I slumped against him. "You're right."

"I'll take you home in an hour, okay? But now, finish up that margarita. You're gonna need it, sweetheart."

Earl was more right than he knew. When we pulled up to the house in my brother's car, I saw my little Lhasa Apso,

Fuzzy, darting back and forth across the lawn. The front door was wide open.

"Oh, no," I breathed.

Inside, our house looked like a war zone. The whole kitchen was torn apart. The beautiful crystal wine glasses Jeremy had bought me for our anniversary lay smashed on the floor. Plates and mugs had joined them. All the coats had been torn out of the front closet. It looked like my fur coat had been stomped on by dirty boots.

The rest of the house was much the same. There was a knife slash through my favorite painting. The coffee table had been overturned; one leg was splintered and ragged. Perfume bottles had been swept onto the bathroom floor. Everything that was mine, or ours, was destroyed, scattered around like so much trash.

Jeremy was nowhere in sight.

I pulled Fuzzy into my arms. He burrowed into the crook of my elbow, shaking. "Take me to Mom and Dad's house," I told my brother. "I can't stay here."

I knew that Jeremy was selfish, but I hadn't fully appreciated the scope of his self-absorption until now.

It didn't matter that we'd been fighting almost daily for months. It didn't matter that he wasn't in love with me anymore—and had told me so on numerous occasions. What mattered was that I'd stopped loving him, and that was unacceptable. Trashing the house was his way of making sure that I suffered as much as he was suffering.

The next morning, I called the house, and Jeremy answered.

"I'm leaving," he told me. "I need a ride to the airport."

"Great," I sighed, not bothering to hide my relief. "That's great."

I think he'd been expecting a different reaction. "You're just going to let me go? You are one cold bitch, Rebecca."

That was exactly how I felt: cold. My marriage was shattered as irrevocably as the crystal glasses Jeremy had smashed on the kitchen floor—but the cracks had been there for a long time. If I hadn't been so attached to the idea of what we were as a couple, I might have noticed them sooner.

My father volunteered to deliver Jeremy and his suitcases to the airport, since I wasn't in any shape to do it myself. Jeremy went to Chicago for a while, then California. I moved back to New York, got a place in Gramercy Park, and tried to disentangle myself from the threads of our old life.

As time passed, I found that I didn't really miss Jeremy. By the end, the only thing we had in common was our shared delusion of grandeur, and that was too flimsy a thing to hold our marriage together. I'd gotten what I thought I'd desired—a handsome husband and a modeling agency—but it hadn't been what I expected.

Turns out, a lot of things are like that. Most of what we desire, we desire because it holds a lesson for us, if we're willing to learn it. I needed to realize that beauty and glamour are only skin deep. My fascination with the superficial was an obstacle to my spiritual growth—a brick in my baggage, so to speak.

When we become entangled with the objects of our desires, it can really mess us up. Our choices become limited, our scope narrowed, because anything which negates the desire (or makes the desire secondary to other considerations) is no longer an option. We make choices we wouldn't normally make, do things we wouldn't normally do, because the fulfillment of our desire has become more important than anything else in our experience.

Such was the case with husband number two.

CHAPTER SEVEN

The New Illusion

"You must choose between your

attachments and happiness."

~ Adyashanti

After Jeremy and I divorced, I spent a few months "finding my way through the dark," as they say. Nothing I'd experienced had been what I expected to find. All my illusions about beauty and glamour had been shattered—but it was still hard to shed my attachments to them.

Who was Rebecca Tripp, anyway? A stewardess, of course. But besides that? Who was I without my big shot husband? Who was I without my modeling agency and my quasi-celebrity status? I'd perceived myself as totally independent within my marriage, but now that Jeremy was gone I realized just how much I'd relied on him to supply my sense of place in the world.

It's disturbingly easy for the human mind to get attached to fame and success. We are all different and unique—but there's a fine line between knowing you're unique and thinking that you're *better*. Jeremy had long since crossed that line. In fact, his psychiatrist officially pegged him as a narcissist (a diagnosis which pleased him to no end). I had wavered on that line myself, especially when the perks and privileges started to become commonplace. It put a big grin on my face when people whispered behind their hands and pointed at Jeremy and me on the street. I was flattered to get the best tables at our favorite restaurants, or the best seats for the latest Broadway show. But the celebrity treatment also put a barrier between me and the rest of the world. I started to see myself as one step (or two, or three) above the masses, and I rather liked the view from above.

Once Jeremy was gone, the perks disappeared too. Once again, I was just another lonely girl in the Big Apple.

I wasn't better than anyone; in fact, I didn't feel like anyone at all. I went from being in the limelight to being practically invisible.

Once the bruises to my ego healed, I was able to reflect on my years with Jeremy more objectively. In a way, I'd been on a behind-the-scenes tour of my own life. All of the things I idealized and epitomized had been revealed in a harsh new light. Nothing was as it seemed.

What I thought I wanted hadn't fulfilled me. Therefore, I must have wanted something else all along.

During this time of unraveling, I traveled to Tahoe to meet three girlfriends for a ski weekend. We dressed to the nines, and hit all the best parties. After months of being single, I was itching to get back in the game. But after an hour of batting my eyelashes and wiggling my hips, I discovered that flirting didn't thrill me the way it once had. Instead, I stepped back and watched my friends chase eligible bachelors with a sense of disconnection, even pity. These girls thought they had to land a rich, gorgeous man to be happy—that they weren't worth enough on their own, or that their lives couldn't be complete without a mansion in Malibu and a private jet. I had had the rich husband and the fame (if not the private jet), and in the end, I just wanted out.

Not that I wasn't still attached to my image. Every day, I put on my makeup and my false eyelashes: they were my armor against the world. The 70s were coming to a close, and flying wasn't what it had been in the 60s, but I still considered it one of the most glamorous jobs in on Earth, and by God I was going to look the part! On that ski trip, though, something changed. Watching my girlfriends sashay around like peacocks on parade made me seriously rethink my approach. Knowing that I was more than my body, why was I still so enraptured with my appearance and the game of physical seduction?

Why did glamour still matter so much to me?

I pondered these deep questions over coffee in the resort restaurant. I thought about what my false eyelashes really signified, and why women wore blusher and painted their fingernails. Lifting my gaze from my own perfect manicure, I noticed a woman standing in line at the counter. When she turned around to meet my gaze, I

179

gasped in amazement. She was beautiful. Ageless. Not loud or glitzy, but classic and elegant, like an old Hollywood movie star. Her skin was flawless, her hair dark and shiny. I couldn't help myself: I kept staring as she ordered her coffee. This woman was... perfect. She was what all of my giggling, gossiping roommates dreamed of being.

And then, as she glided by my table, I happened to glance down at her hands.

It was like she'd tossed ice water in my face. How could such weathered, wrinkled, spotty hands belong to such a radiant woman?

Back in the day, only the wealthiest women underwent cosmetic surgery. It wasn't done often—and when it was, no one talked about it. It wasn't something to be proud of: rather, it was an admission that you'd failed to age gracefully. Procedures tended toward the subtle rather than the extreme. Honestly, if the woman had been wearing gloves, I might have continued to be fooled by the illusion of perfection she presented. But the contrast between hands and face was too marked to be natural.

While her face was captivating, it wasn't enough to disguise the fact that she'd altered herself.

I sank back into thought. Obviously, her looks were important enough to this woman that she felt compelled to cut away bits of her body, stretch and rearrange them, in order to better conform to an ideal. It seemed shallow to me, and more than a little sad—but in a way, I was doing the very same thing. I had no plans to go under the knife, but every day I altered my appearance with lipstick, blusher, false eyelashes, control-top pantyhose…

On the flight home, I studied my face in the mirror in the cramped airline bathroom. Good cheekbones, full mouth. Golden-brown eyes framed by the dense black fringe of my false eyelashes. But I was more than just a pretty face, and I didn't want the artifice anymore.

Grasping one long lash, I peeled off my falsies for the last time. Where they rested in my palm, they looked silly, flimsy—and yet, I'd been attached to them for so long. Every morning of my adult life, I'd carefully glued them in place. I'd never worked a flight without them. They had been my trademark as a modeling agent, and the reason Jeremy first talked to me.

With a sigh, I tossed them in the trash. I was through faking it.

Attachments and Aversions

In the Gospel of Matthew, there's a story about Jesus and a rich young man. In it, the young man asked Jesus what actions would grant him eternal life. Jesus advised the man to obey the Commandments. When the man replied that he already observed them, Jesus told him: "If you want to be perfect, go, sell your possessions and give them to the poor, and you will have treasure in heaven. Then come, follow me."

When the young man heard this, he became very upset. He was, after all, a man of great wealth; why should he give away *everything* that he had amassed? Jesus said, "Indeed, it is easier for a camel to go through the eye of a needle than for a rich man to enter the kingdom of God."

The barrier standing between the rich young man and Heaven wasn't his wealth. Abundance is our birthright as divine beings. The barrier was his *attachment* to his wealth, and the fact that he placed more importance on riches in this dimension than on his connection to his God and eventual ascension.

You don't have to believe in Heaven and Hell to see the merit in this cautionary tale. In order to connect with the infinite, divine spark within yourself, you need to get over your attachments, put down your baggage... and just lighten up.

I'd rid myself of my false eyelashes, but my other attachments were harder to identify, given that they weren't (quite literally) staring me in the face. While married to Jeremy, I got a taste of what being a successful, in-demand business owner could feel like. I was through with the modeling industry, but I wanted to recreate the sense of power and excitement that came with managing a bustling office.

I launched a jewelry business with a model I knew, but it didn't take off the way we'd both hoped. It was fun while it lasted, but my heart wasn't in it.

And that's when I realized a startling truth: I was finally getting tired of New York.

The city had, for many years, had a hold over me. Living there was almost an addiction. After Manhattan, every other place seemed unsophisticated and one-dimensional. Even my stints in California had been short-lived. Besides, who would I be if I left? I was as attached to the title of "New Yorker" as I was to the city itself. But I was also burned out—tired of the constant noise and motion, tired of feeling like an ant in a sea of other ants, all scrabbling over one another on their way to the top of the anthill.

One icy January day, I woke up alone in my Gramercy Park apartment with a strange hollowness inside me, like a vacuum. It wasn't a negative energy, just a great, endless emptiness. Then, a deep, kind, male voice spoke from out of thin air somewhere to my left.

"You will be leaving New York by the end of March," it said.

I wasn't freaked out by this disembodied voice at all. In fact, I was comforted. This was confirmation of what I had already suspected: the Big Apple was no longer my heart's home.

That morning, I called my landlord, who lived in Florida, and asked if I could break my lease. Of course, he said no (even in New York, good tenants are hard to find). I shrugged and went on with my day. If I was meant to leave, something would come up. I could always trust the Universe to provide a solution.

A month later, in mid-February, I got a phone call from that selfsame landlord. "You need to move out by the end of March," he said. "The building is going co-op. I want to buy the apartment, but I can't do it if you're there. Apparently, they want 'owner-occupied.'"

I got a little flutter in my belly. The voice had been right after all.

I headed north to Boston, and bought a condo on the corner of Dartmouth and Newbury Street, right at Copley Place. Now that I didn't have to shepherd Jeremy and his ego through every daily task, Boston held a lot more appeal for me. Yes, it was quieter than Manhattan, but now that I wasn't comparing every venue to its counterpart in New York I found a lot of great social spots.

I also made time to dive deeper into the spiritual methodology which had healed my cervical cancer and appendicitis. I chose the location of my condo in part because it was only a few blocks from the First Church of Christ, Scientist—the world headquarters for Christian Science. I'd lost a lot of my metaphysical connection while married to Jeremy, allowing our shared attachments to beauty and fame to pull me away from my spiritual thought patterns. After my healing from cancer, my connection to G.O.D. and the Fourth Dimension had felt innate and easeful; now, it took a lot of concentration to get those iron filings to stand up in my head.

I found a teacher, and took a twelve-day course known as Class Instruction. Every morning, I walked to the Church in my high heels with my books in a satchel over my shoulder. Copley Place was just being completed at that time, and there was a yellow line painted on the sidewalk to direct pedestrians through the construction site. I called it my "Yellow Brick Road." After the course ended, I did more studying at home, but it was great to be connected to a network of spiritual people.

After Copley Place was completed, real estate prices in my neighborhood went through the roof, so I decided to sell up and move back to the coast. I found an apartment in the city of New Bedford, a former whaling port made famous by Herman Melville's *Moby Dick*.

Boston had been far calmer than Manhattan, but New Bedford was really a shock to my system. I lay in bed each night listening to the eerie silence of the street below my window, and wondered if I was the only person awake in the world. Even the streetlights seemed dimmer, somehow. Maybe it was just the absence of neon.

During that time, I did a lot of reevaluating. I was back in tune with the spiritual dimension, and would often receive messages about where to go and what to do on a daily basis. At night, I would dream myself into a classroom, and get a download of new information into my subconscious brain. Sometimes, I would remember what I learned when I woke up, but sometimes it translated simply as a new "knowing."

I'd been on a couple of dates since moving from Boston. Invariably, at some point during dinner, the man would ask me, "What are you doing here?"

"I was sent here," I'd reply, although I wasn't clear why.

With so much new information pouring into me each night, I still struggled to make a decision about my future. Should I stop flying? I was no longer the material girl I had been in my twenties, nor was flying as glamorous as I remembered from those early days. I simply wasn't finding the mental and social stimulation I craved in the air any longer.

"What am I waiting for?" I asked in my prayers. "What is coming my way?"

I got my answer, and, of course, it wasn't what I expected.

If I hadn't been living in New Bedford, Tom would never have found me. I was kind of a sitting duck there, waiting as I was for the next adventure to come along and scoop me up. He called out of the blue and asked if I wanted to have lunch. Curious, I agreed. We'd known one another as teenagers, and I'd always found him charming. He was attractive in a mediocre sort of way: nondescript brown hair, brown eyes, athletic in that rich-boy, tennis-playing way. His personality was definitely on the intense side, and there was a fiery spark in those brown eyes that caught my attention right from the start.

Tom had recently moved back to the East coast from Salt Lake City because his mother had fallen ill. He was totally unapologetic about the fact that he wanted to see what he could grab after she finally called it quits on this plane; they didn't have a very healthy relationship. He was also looking for a partner in his new business venture, which involved reselling telephone time for AT&T and Sprint. The telephone industry had recently been deregulated, and there was big money to be made if you were quick about it.

There was a lot of the con man in Tom; I knew it from the start. But I could sense his genuine excitement about the business, and that was enough to get me interested. I still craved the kind of success I'd had with Jeremy in our modeling agency, and here was Tom, offering precisely that. I jumped on board with barely a second thought.

Tom and I spent a lot of time together that first year, and one thing led to another. We were married in a judge's chambers in Groton, Connecticut, because Tom couldn't find his divorce papers from his first marriage and Connecticut law didn't require us to present them.

There were no guests, no witnesses. Our marriage was really more of a business arrangement: we were partners first, lovers second. It was a silly reason to get married, really. But I was certain that Tom and I were going to make it big together.

I had fallen for the dream. Again.

With Tom's encouragement, I opened a shop in Newport, Rhode Island named Port of Call. I loved to explore the Asian markets on layovers, so it was a natural step for me to bring back clothing and accessories from my visits to China, Japan, and Cambodia. Buying for the store gave me an excuse to keep flying. The store also gave us a secondary stream of income, and a venue through which to solicit new customers for the telephone business.

We moved into a condo on the famous Bellevue Avenue, home of the Newport Mansions. Our home was in Sherwood Mansion, across from Rosecliff. It looked like the White House, all marble and sweeping lawns. The space was already beautifully furnished (courtesy of the last tenant, who was in jail for embezzlement) and more than large enough to accommodate an office for our telephone resale business.

From the outside, everything looked perfect. Tom and I entertained, networked, and schmoozed with all the biggest players in the area, and presented the picture of a happy, dedicated husband and wife team. But on the inside, things were going downhill fast—so fast, in fact, that I began to feel like I was caught in a landslide.

First, the business was far more difficult to run than either of us had anticipated. Small businesses like ours had to put a lot of money in escrow accounts in case our clients didn't pay their phone bills. Back then, there was no computer software to track financial records and sales, so bookkeeping was both time-consuming and stressful. Tom swilled glass after glass of Jack Daniels as he racked his brain for ways to keep the company afloat.

Then, it came to light that the woman who ran Port of Call for me while I was flying had been stealing from the till. That pretty much soured my appetite for the whole venture, and I closed the store just over a year after opening it. Tom and I had to absorb the cost of the merchandise, which put us even further in debt.

It was during this time that I began to see how attachments can really drive people crazy. I met a lot of entrepreneurs during this phase of my life, and what I discovered was that while they were all hustle and bustle during the inception of a business, their insatiable attachment to the creative process made it impossible for them to follow through with the mundane day-to-day running of the businesses they founded. I suppose that's why so many businesses fail in the first couple of years: lack of stimulation. Certainly it was a factor in the downfall of Jeremy's and my modeling agency.

Tom's attachments were different. Like Jeremy, he was entranced by the idea of success. But while Jeremy had been lazy and more than a little entitled, Tom was dead set on making it work no matter what. I could leave on a three-day trip and come home to find him still hunched over his desk, typing furiously on his typewriter, unwashed and unshaven, wearing the same clothes he'd been wearing when I left. He took workaholism to a whole new level.

As his obsession deepened, so did his depression. He also had a violent temper, exacerbated by the Jack Daniels. He turned that temper on me often, lashing out with words until I thought I would bleed. I guess I was just the easiest target.

On the rare occasions when he wasn't working, Tom invited his sister over to our condo, where the two of them spent hours rehashing the worst scenes from their childhoods. Their father died when they were very young, and their mother had apparently been a first-class head case. Every single solitary thing that went wrong in either of their lives could, with enough persistence on their parts, be traced back to something their mother did to them, or in front of them, or within hearing range of them. "Blame therapy," I called it.

From my spot on the sidelines, I could clearly see that Tom was caught in a psychological trap. The memories he hated had become his identity. He thought that being ultra-successful would help him break free of his past, but the more he attached himself to his delusions of grandeur and the overwhelming need to "be someone," the greater the cycle of need he created. His thoughts were focused on escape. He wasn't passionate about the telephone business; he was passionate about being someone other than who he was. But the more he thought about what he wasn't, the more he reinforced the feelings of lack he hated.

When he slipped into one of his depressions, nothing I did or said could snap him out of it. I talked about my high hopes for the business, and all the plans we could make together to turn things around. I told him how we could try to see our situation in a positive light. I told him that G.O.D. would take care of us, if we just trusted in the process. Nothing I said made the slightest bit of difference. In fact, my positive words often sent him into even more violent fits of temper. Flying became my escape; skipping town for days at a time was the only thing that made the situation bearable.

I called dozens of experts, all of whom recommended that Tom be brought to their respective facilities for treatment. Tom refused every suggestion. Finally, I ended up on the phone with a woman at the Hoffman Institute in New York. She spelled out the situation for me in a way that no one else had. "It doesn't matter what your husband does," she said firmly. "It matters what *you* do. If you allow yourself to be controlled by the one who's depressed, you've lost the whole game. He doesn't have dominion over you. His behavior doesn't have to affect you."

She was right, of course. I might not have been sporting bruises, but I was allowing myself to be abused all the same. By trying to coddle Tom, and feeding his delusions in order to have a few hours of peace in our home, I was playing a game I couldn't win. It wasn't my job to fix his issues. If I wanted the situation to change, I had to change my reaction to the situation.

It was my Mother Teresa moment all over again.

It's a strong, strong attachment, this idea that we can change another human being. People go into marriages thinking that they can shape and mold their spouse. They say things like, "If he/she only did *this*, our relationship would be perfect." It takes a lot of strength to accept that we can't choose anyone else's path. If we try, we're actually doing them a disservice, because we're distracting them from the lessons life is presenting.

Being able to accept others for who they truly are is one of the greatest skills we can acquire on this plane. But that doesn't mean that we have to stand there meekly while people throw their bricks at us. Accepting someone fully can also mean accepting that their energy simply isn't aligned with yours. You're walking your own road: you don't have to travel with anyone who makes it harder for you to move forward.

When people are hurting enough to act in destructive, violent, or abusive ways, chances are they'll do their best to take you down with them. In my experience, the more attachments people have, the more destructive they become, because their anger over the way things are (as opposed to how things "should" be) overrides their ability to accept a given situation. Some people stand their ground against rage like that day in and day out—like I did with Tom. But what does it prove? Who gets to move forward in that situation?

In the end, it wasn't love that kept me in my marriage for three long years: I'd never really been in love with Tom, not even at the beginning, and deep down I knew it. What kept me there were my own attachments. I was holding on to the illusion that our business was on the verge of exploding into something exciting and lucrative. I was afraid to disappoint our employees, or leave them out in the cold. More than anything, I was afraid to admit that I had failed in two marriages. I wanted to preserve that sparkling image of success and happiness that Tom and I were still, somehow, managing to present to the outside world.

Then, one day, I awoke to the news that the escrow money was gone. The telephone companies who had been so keen on our business suddenly wanted nothing to do with us. The depression that Tom plunged into that day was more than a downward spiral: it was a freefall. I can see now that he would have ended up there even if the business had succeeded: he was too attached to his misery to live without it for long. My worry for him quickly turned to terror of him. I couldn't predict what would set him off, especially when he was drinking. I started taking more flying jobs, just to get out of his reach.

It was my fear of Tom that finally allowed me to let go of my attachment to the dream of successful entrepreneurship. The price was simply too high. I had to get away.

I started making moves toward separation, but Tom wasn't going to let me go that easily. I was like a possession to him: in his mind, he owned me. And without the telephone business to consume all that mental intensity, I became his new obsession.

While he was out one afternoon, I packed up my clothes and some knickknacks and escaped to my parents' house in Westport. I left everything else behind: there was nothing in that opulent house I wanted. Every possession we shared—every chair, every table, every glass and platter— seemed tainted somehow, like it had been scorched black by Tom's rage.

For a couple of days, the phone was silent. Then, Tom called to ask me to meet him at a restaurant in Newport. He said he wanted to talk about tax fallout from the collapse of the business.

Warily, I agreed.

Throughout the meal, he was despondent and edgy. The tax discussion had taken all of five minutes; after that, the conversation grew awkward and stilted. I couldn't wait to get out of there, but I couldn't seem to manufacture an excuse to leave.

Over dessert, he caught my hand across the table and said, "I have to be with you. I can't live without you." His eyes were terribly intense.

"You're going to have to learn," I told him, hoping my nervousness didn't show. "I'm not coming back, Tom."

I paid the bill, of course, as he must have known I would. He made a show of walking me to my car. He was parked right behind me on Thames Street. As I drove off, I felt relieved that he hadn't tried to kiss me or manhandle me. Actually, aside from all the "woe is me" stuff, he'd been pretty well-behaved.

And then, I glanced in the rearview mirror and saw that he was tailing me.

He was driving erratically, swerving from one side of the lane to the other, his front bumper sometimes coming within inches of my trunk. I drove faster, but he kept up with me. Finally, I made a tire-squealing turn into the parking lot at Second Beach. Two men were standing under a streetlight, smoking cigarettes and chatting. Throwing myself out of the car, I latched onto one man's arm and started babbling incoherently.

"He's going to kill me. You have to call the police... Please! Please call them!"

The guy to whom I hadn't glued myself gave me a quizzical look, but he dashed off to the nearest phone booth to call 9-1-1. By then, Tom had pulled into the parking lot. He got out of his car, totally nonchalant in his expensive suit and designer shoes. I knew what came next. He was going to play the patient, long-suffering husband—the very personification of reason and logic— while framing me as the crazy, over-emotional wife. I could practically smell the bullshit he was cooking up.

I held onto that strange man's arm and refused to say a word until the police showed up.

"He was following me," I told them. "We're in the middle of a divorce, and I'm afraid he's going to run me off the road. Please don't let him follow me home!"

Of course, Tom couldn't come up with a good reason why he was there in the parking lot, or why he'd been tailing me when his condo was in the total opposite direction. Plus, he smelled like booze, and was almost certainly over the legal limit. The police ended up holding him for the night. I drove myself home, shaking so hard my teeth were chattering.

Unfortunately, that wasn't the last I saw of Tom. Whether I was in Westport, Newport, or anywhere in between, he'd suddenly materialize beside me in his shiny sports car. He would sometimes tail me for miles—not aggressively, like that first night, but as if he wanted to see where I was going. There were notes left on my windshield, random visits while I was sitting in the dentist's chair (now *that* was weird; I almost choked on a piece of gauze!) and multiple "chance" encounters at gas stations, grocery stores, salons…

One night, after working a late flight into Boston, I pulled into my parents' driveway to find the house and yard shrouded in shadow. This was unusual; my mother always left an outside light on for me. As I opened the car door, the handle was yanked out of my hand—and there he was, dressed all in black. He had been hiding in the bushes like a sniper.

I was convinced that he had murdered my parents. They were harboring a fugitive—me—and he had made them pay. It was all I could do not to start screaming.

Somehow, I talked him into letting me into the house, where I called 9-1-1. Thankfully, my parents were fine (when Tom realized what I was doing, he let loose his usual verbal stream of vitriol, and my parents stumbled downstairs in their bathrobes to find out what was going on) but after that night my already constant fear was ratcheted up another several notches.

I took out a restraining order against him. It didn't do any good. Everywhere I went, Tom was there. Whether I was in Europe, Alaska, or Hong Kong, he would find me. I got calls in hotel rooms, in airports, even at restaurants. Once, in Anchorage, I told the hotel desk not to put through any calls. In the morning, I found out he'd called seventeen times. It became my practice to unplug the telephone the minute I set foot in my hotel room. I felt like I was under siege.

My flying partners were as confused and freaked out by this as I was. How was Tom getting my schedule? Was it just floating around out there for anyone to find? Then, it came to light that another stewardess was feeding Tom my flight information. With that classic con man charm of his, he'd convinced this girl that *I* was the nut. I can just imagine the lies he cooked up about his poor, deranged ex-wife, so unhinged by his leaving that she was borderline suicidal. He was keeping track of me for my own safety, of course. Poor little Rebecca, all alone without her big, strong man to take care of her.

Part of me wanted to warn this girl what she was messing with, but I knew she wouldn't believe a word I said. She was probably more than half in love with Tom already. He was that slick.

The harassing phone calls got so out of control that they caught the attention of my superiors. If the calls didn't stop, I was told, I would find myself out of a job. I think Tom's little spy got a talking to, too, because things quieted down a bit—but nothing was going to stop Tom from getting to me. Even without a helper to do his dirty work, he managed to find me several times a week. I started sleeping on friends' floors and couches, just to avoid going home.

Finally, some friends in New York took pity on me, and set me up with an off-the-books sublet on the Upper West Side. For six months, I went completely underground. I made no unnecessary phone calls, received no mail, and never left the apartment except to go to the airport. I refused to give United my forwarding information. My parents knew I was in New York, but even they didn't have my actual address.

During those few months, I was always looking over my shoulder. I jumped at every noise, and barely slept. What made it worse was the fact that Tom was so... average. Whereas I could have spotted Jeremy in a crowd of thousands, Tom could blend in anywhere. I thought I saw him on the street a hundred times a day—only to look closer and find I was gaping at a stranger.

To top it all off, I was forced to declare bankruptcy. The failed telephone resale business had drained every last penny of my savings. I could barely live on my airline salary.

All my dreams of success, all my definitions of myself, had been shattered. I was an abused woman running for her life with nothing but the clothes on her back.

Real change happens when we let go of all the things we thought had the power to define us. There's a metaphysical solution to every problem we face as human beings—but in order to find it, we have to go deep within ourselves, past our attachments and expectations, past our hopes and wishes for ourselves and the people in our lives. Only when the slate is completely blank—when we've handed all our riches over to G.O.D., like the young man in the story—can we start to rewrite our reality.

I most definitely wasn't there yet.

CHAPTER EIGHT

You Might Need a Private Jet

"Lay not up for yourselves treasures upon

Earth, where moth and rust doth corrupt, and

where thieves break through and steal. But lay

up for yourselves treasures in Heaven, where

neither moth nor rust doth corrupt, and where

thieves do not break through nor steal."

~ Matthew 6:19-20

During the time I was underground in New York, the murder of Nicole Simpson, the late wife of football superstar O.J. Simpson, was all over the news. I found myself relating to her situation too closely for comfort. It wouldn't have taken much, I realized, to push Tom to that kind of violence. If I'd stayed in Westport, it might have come to that. But Nicole didn't have the options I did: she was too famous, too recognizable. She couldn't just disappear into the crowds of the Upper West Side. I might have had to give up my life as I knew it—but she had given up her life, period.

It was profound for me to realize that despite the overwhelming fear and uncertainty I was living with, I was actually a very lucky woman.

Over the course of six months, Tom's harassing phone calls slowed, then finally stopped completely. I still didn't feel altogether safe on the street, but I had the strong sense that Tom had moved on. Maybe he'd found another victim; maybe he'd latched onto another crazy business venture. I didn't know, and didn't care. All I knew was that my intuition was telling me it was safe to come out of hiding.

Back at my parents' house in Westport, I was restless, casting around for something to keep my mind from straying into fearfulness. Since getting together with Tom, I'd taken a big step back in terms of metaphysical thinking. My mind had reverted to the materially-based thought processes of dollars and cents, success and failure. I'd even lost touch with my daily practices of prayer and creative visualization. More, I couldn't seem to locate the sense of security that had carried me through so many other challenging experiences. I had no control over Tom's thoughts or actions, and that made me feel terribly vulnerable. I couldn't leave him behind the way I had my rapist in Jamaica. I struggled to come back into the perfect understanding I'd experienced after my healing from cancer—but it was like trying to catch a cloud with a butterfly net. Every time I glimpsed that lightness, it just slipped through my fingers.

So, I decided to stop struggling and go with the flow. With my toes dug firmly into the material realm, I opened an antiques consignment shop called The Junk Box. Looking back, the name seems doubly appropriate: maybe I was subconsciously trying to clean out my own baggage by selling off other people's stuff.

The shop was an immediate success. I started getting consignments from people in Westport, Newport, and the surrounding area. Soon, collectors were popping in to peruse my wares on a regular basis—including one local man whose interest, it quickly became clear, went beyond Queen Anne dressers and Art Deco chandeliers.

Michael Cushing was the exact opposite of my ex-husband, Tom. Where Tom had been driven by the need to succeed, Michael was a trust fund baby, and appeared totally at ease with his own affluence. Where Tom had been manic, Michael was laid-back. He believed that if he just waited long enough, the world would eventually make its way to his doorstep.

As the months went on, Michael stopped by The Junk Box more and more frequently. He was funny and charming, and, while not as handsome as either of my ex-husbands, he was attractive in a rugged sort of way. He'd been a military man once upon a time, and it still showed in his bearing.

From what I could tell, Michael wanted many of the same things I did: a comfortable home, from where he could pursue his interests in antiques and history; a comfortable lifestyle that allowed him to do whatever he wanted, whenever he wanted; and a comfortable relationship where both parties were at ease with one another. After a year or so of dating, he told me that I was the person with whom he wanted to share this vision.

The love I had for Michael wasn't the breathless, almost worshipful love I'd had for Jeremy at first; it wasn't passionate or consuming. Nor did we have the dream of whirlwind success that drew Tom and me together. What Michael and I had was a deeper, more satisfying version of friendship. It was comfortable, like an old sweater. Our marriage was something I could sink into with a sigh of relief.

Those first few years were wonderful. Michael had a bawdy sense of humor, and he could always make me laugh. We traveled a lot together as well, and while he wasn't the adventurer I was, it was nice to hold his hand as we strolled the moonlit streets of Paris.

Turbulence

On one coast-to-coast flight in the 1970s, our DC-8 hit a really rough patch of turbulence over the Rocky Mountains. The plane's wings were bouncing and flexing as they're built to do, but the rattling was so fierce that it felt like the plane was being torn apart at the seams. I had to sit down in one of the passenger seats and buckle up. Looking out over the wing, I saw the rivets that held the wings together jumping up and down, like they were going to leap right out of their sockets.

I knew there was a good chance that things could get dangerous. If the wing came apart, we would fall out of the sky, and there was nothing I could do. Big chunks of my life flashed before my eyes. It was like a movie; a jagged sequence of scenes, one after the other. They weren't good, or bad, they just were. As these vignettes unfolded, a profound peace descended upon me. Death wasn't something to fear: it was nothing more than a peaceful transition from sleeping to waking. The iron filings in my head started tingling, and I knew that wherever I went after I stepped out of my "spacesuit," it would be the perfect place for me. These scenes from this life would be with me, like dreams lingering in my mind long into the morning—but in the end, they would be just that: dreams.

After that, no mid-air turbulence could shake me. Even when conditions had passengers in panicked tears, I remained perfectly calm.

It's been said that all fear ultimately stems from the fear of death. Our fears about violence, lack, abandonment, and disease can all be traced back to that one ultimate fear. For me, the key to being comfortable with death was accepting that I am not my body. If the truest part of me is pure, eternal spirit, nothing that happens to this body— up to and including death—can truly harm *me*. Injury, disease, aging... None of these can touch me, because I have no fear of them.

During my marriage to Tom, I lost a lot of that certainty. My fear of death returned full-force, disguised as fear of violence and powerlessness. Being with Michael helped me get centered and grounded again. His presence was earthy and solid, and in his shelter I felt protected enough to shed those layers of negativity. The process of returning to my spiritual self took several years, but by the time death found me again, I was ready to look it in the face without cringing.

In mid-August 2001, I put in my bid to fly United Airlines Flight 175 from Boston to Los Angeles on the morning of September 11.

Shortly thereafter, my friend Brian called, and suggested that I change my bid. It wasn't unusual for me to receive such a call. United Airlines had prearranged contracts with thousands of hotels, and each contract was tied to a flight. When you chose your flight, you also chose your layover hotel. Brian had just laid over at a hotel in Santa Monica that was much nicer than the one attached to Flight 175.

"You could make it a spa weekend," he suggested.

I loved the idea. So I changed my schedule, and departed Boston on September 10 instead.

In the early morning hours of September 11, I watched the news coverage of the terrorist attacks from my hotel bed in a strange state of suspended reality. The footage of Flight 175 crashing into the North Tower flashed across the screen. The impact. The flames. The collapse. The screams. Over and over, like snapshots of a nightmare.

If it hadn't been for Brian's phone call, I would have been on that flight.

After my initial shock wore off, the fact that death had brushed my shoulder didn't really faze me. Maybe if I hadn't already been so immersed in the process of regaining my spiritual security, my near-miss would have been a wake-up call; as it was, this was just confirmation of everything I knew to be true. When my work here in this three-dimensional world was done, my higher self would choose the proper time and place to set aside my human body—but until that time arrived, I was totally protected. There was no sense getting caught up in the what-ifs.

Meanwhile, in Los Angeles, things were rapidly devolving into chaos. No one knew what was going on. Despite my near miss, I was the calmest of anyone present, so I was recruited to interface with the United offices to find out how the heck we Stews were going to get out of L.A. Amtrak was totally booked, and although I could rent a car, I wouldn't have been allowed to cross state lines. The whole nation was under suspicion, but anyone tied to the airlines was doubly scrutinized.

That first week, it took forever to get an answer about anything. No one wanted to make a decision for fear it would be the wrong one. The terror was thicker than Los Angeles smog, and just as pervasive. But I also witnessed the way that people banded together to get things done, and reached out to one another for support in a way I'd never seen before.

All week long, I heard stories of how people had narrowly missed being on Flights 175 and 11. One man I met in a coffee shop had flown to L.A. a day early because his colleague changed his ticket without asking him. "I was totally ticked off that I had to change my travel plans at the last minute," he told me, speaking slowly through a haze of guilt and relief. "But he literally saved my life." More amazing stories were circulating: others whose flight plans had changed unexpectedly, executives with offices in the World Trade Center who became inexplicably ill and couldn't go to work, people who missed their usual bus or train, people who decided on a whim to turn down a different street. There was a rhythm to these stories, it seemed; a synchronicity too big to be mere coincidence. Each of these survivors had a purpose yet to be fulfilled. Their higher selves had *chosen* for them to live.

What I started pondering, as the days wore on, was why everyone on Flight 175 had chosen to die. One young flight attendant I knew had been on board with his soon-to-be-wife. He had told me once, in awed tones, how naturally spiritual his fiancée was, and how everyone loved to be in her presence. He himself had toyed with the idea of an ascetic life, but felt he could serve the world better by living as part of society. Why, I wondered, had a couple with so much to share chosen, however unconsciously, to end their time here? And yet, clearly, they had.

By Friday of that week, the airports were (sort of) operational again, and my colleagues and I were able to head back to the East Coast. We would be forced to land in Manchester, New Hampshire, because Boston's Logan Airport was still considered a crime scene—but I didn't care about the extra hours of travel time. I wanted out of L.A.

Boarding that flight was eerie, surreal. Everyone was on high alert, buzzing with fear and adrenaline. I walked up to the cockpit to say hello to the pilot—but I was in civilian clothes, and although the whole crew knew who I was they wouldn't let me past the cockpit door. Before takeoff, the police removed one first-class passenger because he was "acting strangely." To me, the guy just looked jittery—as anyone might, having just gone through the hellish new security screening at LAX.

After 9/11, I flew for only one more year. I didn't leave the sky because I was afraid: even terrorists didn't have the power to scare me off the job. But the joy I'd always found in flying had disappeared. I couldn't continue to live a metaphysical life in the sky when I was being ordered by my employer and the government to act fearful and paranoid. After I had to attend a class where I and my fellow Stews watched videos detailing how to kill an intruder with our bare hands, I handed in my resignation. I had no desire to learn to hate the job I'd loved for thirty-five years.

The autumn of 2001 was a time of major turbulence. Even for those who didn't personally know someone affected by the 9/11 attacks, fear became a daily companion. The unrest of the time, fueled by the media and the government, fed prejudices and racial hatreds, and undermined all of that cooperative energy I'd witnessed initially. I watched the people I knew become distrustful and paranoid. People wouldn't get on airplanes for fear that they, too, might become victims of terrorism. Emotional baggage buried deep in people's subconscious minds came flying up to the surface, providing the raw materials for more and more of those proverbial bricks. What might have been a time of increased faith and spiritual connection became just the opposite, as people let their fears about death and violence put more and more barriers between themselves and the divine love and trust of the Fourth Dimension.

I recognized this fear as the same fear Tom had instilled in me, and which I conquered through my slow reconnection to my highest self and G.O.D. When I was ready to retire my flight suit at last, it was this recognition which helped to push me toward my greatest path—the path of a teacher and healer.

The Path Less Traveled

After my retirement, I frittered around Westport, looking for something to do. Nothing seemed to fit me anymore. Like a gawky teenager, I'd outgrown my old life, but wasn't quite ready to step into a new one. I thought about opening another antiques shop, but the idea didn't excite me. I applied for reception jobs at high-end spas and restaurants, but nothing came through. It wasn't like I needed to work—Michael had oodles of money from his trust fund, and wasn't afraid to spend it—but I was used to the constant stimulation of life in the sky, and being grounded in the small community of Westport was *beyond* boring.

This emotional fidgeting went on for nearly two years. I was in a personal Purgatory, waiting for a ray of light to shine down and pull me out of the grayness. Searching for answers, I delved even more deeply into metaphysics, and reconnected with many of the studies and practices in which I'd been dabbling when I first met Jeremy.

One day, I popped into a metaphysical bookstore called Be Here Now in Bristol, Rhode Island. The owner was having a storewide clearance sale to make room for new inventory. I grabbed any title that looked even the least bit interesting, and left with a towering pile.

The first book on the pile was *The Silva Method* by José Silva. I was only mildly interested when I opened the cover, but the book soon had my full attention. Contained within those pages was a detailed description of everything I'd been practicing—both consciously and subconsciously— since Ron Schauff taught me creative visualization back in 1967! Every word spoke to me loud and clear, like a message straight from G.O.D. That night, I fully remembered that I didn't have to wait around for something to show me the way out of my grayness—all I had to do was decide what I wanted, and use the power of my thought to create it!

In the back of *The Silva Method* was a supplemental page advertising for Silva UltraMind trainers. I called the telephone number listed there, and ended up speaking with a man in New York for over an hour. A few months later, in March, I flew to Miami to participate in my first metaphysical training workshop.

I later described my trainer as "the gargoyle at the door of the temple." He was the guardian of life-changing information, and took his teaching very seriously—but he oozed machismo, and would make off-color jokes to the women in the group without a second thought. He also had a tendency to mutter, which made him really hard to understand. Several people left after the end of the first day, unable to stifle their reactions to his, um, unusual personality. I liked him despite his hard edges; after being a Stew for so many years, his silly sexist comments just rolled right off my back.

By the end of that first week, I and the remaining students came to see that the messenger didn't matter nearly as much as the message. I could feel my thought process transitioning from objective—attached to the physical world—to subjective, or inward-focused. I truly began to understand that every single thought had the power to affect my life and how I functioned in it. I'd always been great at creative visualization, but I hadn't paid much attention to the thoughts that floated through my head over the course of an average day. Now, I saw a whole bunch of suitcases that needed to be unpacked and sorted.

I returned to Westport with a renewed sense of purpose. The internal inventory I conducted over the next several months was intense, and often painful. I unpacked and examined my entire relationship with Tom, and my marriage to Jeremy. It was revealed to me that my constant desire for adventure and stimulation attracted unstable personalities to my experience. Beyond even my two previous husbands, I'd encountered a lot of kooky people in my life—from creepy Guy the building manager, to cheating Robert, to the squatter and thieving neighbors in Jeremy's loft—and I had manifested every single one of them because my greatest desire was not to be bored.

I also discovered that I was a natural teacher. I'd been informally teaching passengers and my fellow Stews for years, simply by living my truth. I wondered: why not take that natural communication to the next level?

That May, I taught my first Silva UltraMind workshop to an amazing group of twelve people. It was easy and natural for me to speak about the power of thought, and the infinite potential of the Fourth Dimension and the spiritual mind. My students responded to this information with just as much enthusiasm, joy, and relief as I had. We were taking our power back from the unreliable hands of our own untutored thought, and paving the way to the lives we truly desired.

With that first success under my belt, I launched myself into my new career with a passion I hadn't felt since my early days of flying. I traveled around the country teaching Silva UltraMind workshops, giving people the creative visualization and thought control tools they needed to change their lives. Over and over, I watched people take what seemed like an inescapably negative situation and turn it on its head. One of my students cured herself of fibromyalgia simply by changing her thought. Another manifested the business deal of a lifetime. Others drew new cars, new homes, and new relationships into their lives with an ease and grace they'd never experienced before.

It was during this time—while my new career was expanding literally at the speed of thought—that things started to go downhill with Michael.

The Baby Elephant

When we were first married, I moved into Michael's historic house by the water. As with many period homes in New England, the rooms were small, and the windows oddly-sized and often drafty. I thought Michael would want to stay there forever, given his love for all things antique—but shortly before I retired from flying, he surprised me.

"We should build a new house," Michael announced as I dragged myself through the door after an overnight flight from California. "We can make it exactly how we want it. Imagine! We can have a big Jacuzzi tub in the master bathroom, and a patio for entertaining, and a walk-in closet…"

In my exhaustion, I quickly lost track of all the things we "could have," but I smiled and nodded as he rambled on. I had never seen Michael this animated before. It was kind of nice to know that my normally placid husband had this kind of fire in him.

His passion for our dream house also translated into passion of another sort. He literally swept me off my feet in a way he hadn't done since our wedding night.

Over the next few months, Michael threw himself into the building project. He seemed to have boundless energy. Our new home became almost as powerful an obsession for him as the telephone business had been for Tom. I would wake up in the middle of the night to find

Michael poring over schematics, making notes about the dimensions of rooms or the placement of kitchen cabinets. There wasn't anything in our new house about which he didn't have some input, right down to the brand of screws the contractors used for the sheet rock. He drove the architects crazy.

It was at this point that I began to feel something was wrong. I mean, anyone would have been excited about the home we were building; the place was going to be fabulous. But it seemed that the house had become far, far more important to Michael than the actual living we were going to do in it.

Finally, the big day came. At the unveiling, Michael was like a little kid, bouncing around the empty, echoing rooms with a manic grin on his face. I was excited too— but there was still that nagging sense that something was off. I told myself it would all be okay. Now that the work was done and our dream home was finally a reality, things would go back to normal.

A year later, it was clear that normal was far behind us.

Immediately after our move, Michael transferred his obsession with building to an obsession with decorating. He bought antiques from all over the world, and crowded our rooms with beautiful but crazily mismatched furniture. It was like living in a museum where the curator has dementia. We ended up with four bureaus for the guest bedroom, because he had somehow "forgotten" that he'd purchased the first three. There were Japanese vases crowded onto Shaker side tables beside Victorian sofas. An extra bedroom was designated as the "storage closet"; you couldn't even walk through the space, it was so packed with furniture.

Other issues, too, were rapidly coming to light. A veteran of the Vietnam War, Michael struggled intermittently with nightmares and flashbacks. He might have been diagnosed with PTSD, if I'd ever been able to get him to go to a therapist. When he couldn't sleep, he would wander the house, running his fingers over all of his treasured antiques, as if feeling their expensive solidity comforted him. (I was powerfully reminded of Jeremy, bent over his modeling portfolio in the dead of night, tracing the contours of his own face on the pages.)

If the house tour didn't work, Michael dug into his stash of high-octane prescription meds and knocked himself out cold.

By the time Michael's mania revealed itself, I was fully invested in my career as a Silva UltraMind trainer. My sight was clearer than it had been in a long time, so rather than get reactive about this disturbing turn of events, I took a mental step back from my marriage and tried to see what was actually happening.

I saw that my husband was imprisoned by his belongings. He clung to them like a drowning man clings to driftwood. But they were never enough. How could they be? Stuff is never a substitute for substance. Every new acquisition generated a feeling of happiness in him for a while, but nothing kept him feeling full. I don't know where this vast, sucking need came from; maybe it was a product of his childhood, which had been filled with cruel manipulation and emotional abuse. But despite the fact that his possessions clearly weren't making him happy, my husband continued to chase them with fierce determination.

Michael's obsession with things expanded to include the money he needed to buy those things. He made a lot of reckless investments with his trust fund, and lost a great deal of money. I'm talking millions. As his bank accounts shrank, Michael didn't just continue to spend: he spent *more.*

In my head, I started to refer to him as "the Baby Elephant." He was crashing along on some crazy quest to find his mama, flattening whatever was in his path. He wasn't looking for his real mother, but rather for the emotional nurturing he needed but hadn't received as a child. At the same time, he clutched onto his material possessions with the ferocity of a toddler clutching his blanket. It was probably the most extreme example of physical baggage I've ever seen.

So many people I know are attached to their stuff and their lifestyles. Call it "quality of life" all you want—but when your need to live The Good Life keeps you up at night, or directs you to make decisions that aren't in alignment with your conscience or intuition, then what you're living isn't The Good Life anymore. If you spend more time worrying about your things than you do enjoying them, they have become baggage. Other aspects of lifestyle, or how we show up in the world, are also common and destructive attachments: the need to have a mate, the need to be respected, the need to be smarter than everyone else in the room.

When I turned that clear sight on myself, I saw that I was attached, too. Even though metaphysics was now my full-time pursuit, I still got stressed out—especially when Michael was in one of his manic states. When I felt panicky, I would take an inventory in my mind: "I have a husband who loves me. I have a beautiful home. I go out with my friends. I buy beautiful things." I'd run through my list over and over, trying to reassure myself that my life was working—that I'd manifested everything I'd ever hoped for, just as I taught people to do in my workshops. But deep down I knew that the laundry list of "good things" wasn't enough to fulfill me, any more than pretty baubles were enough to fulfill my floundering husband.

The deeper I sank into my own introspection, the harder it became for me to look at my life and see it as acceptable. Michael's attachments, neuroses, and prescription drug use were not only harmful to him: they were harmful to me. It was an ongoing struggle to keep my thought elevated when his destructive behavior was so firmly entrenched. I wasn't angry at him for being who he was; I still loved him. But we no longer valued the same things. I was growing beyond him—and the higher I flew, the more clearly I saw.

After twelve years of marriage to Michael, the time finally came for me to get out from under the Baby Elephant. Part of me was afraid to leave, knowing that I'd be living on nothing more than my meager airline pension and the revenue from my workshops. I'd have to make a lot of budget cuts, and change a lot of expensive habits. But if I *didn't* shed those attachments, I was going to stay miserable and stressed out.

And so it was that I found myself on my own again, at the tail end of marriage number three, with almost as few material possessions as I'd had when I started. But this time, it was all okay. In fact, it was more than okay. I was starting at square one, and this time I was going to create my life *exactly* the way I wanted it.

What "The Good Life" Really Looks Like

I believe that we choose our life experiences from the Fourth Dimension before we even arrive here on Earth. Our circumstances, our encounters, even our physical bodies are preselected. They are the raw materials we use to grow and develop our souls. Sometimes, these choices are karmic in nature, a way of "paying back" the wrongs of our actions in past lives; sometimes they're for other reasons. And sometimes, if we manage to set aside our baggage and reflect upon our lives with loving objectivity, we even get to know what those reasons are.

Whatever adventure we're launched into at birth is the right one for us. Even people born into dire circumstances of poverty, abuse, or neglect choose that experience before entering their earthly bodies. On a human level, it's hard to encompass. Why would anyone *choose* to live with such pain? But on a fourth-dimensional level, every experience is a lesson in life's classroom. The hardest tests present the greatest opportunities for growth. How can we know compassion if we've never known suffering? How can we appreciate love or abundance if we've never felt their lack? Our task isn't to stop all suffering, but transform our suffering into something beautiful: a compassionate strength that serves the whole world.

What we value, and what we despise, defines us. Our attachments and aversions are part of our emotional baggage, but they're subtle. Attachments don't happen because the things we're attached to are healthy for us. Attachments happen because of our aversions—our deepest fears, the things we don't want to look at because they're so terrifying. Whatever we're attached to, chances are we're in aversion to its opposite.

Aversions and fears limit our choices, and keep us stuck until we identify them and rid ourselves of their corresponding attachments. No matter how we avoid confronting our stuff, it keeps showing up. If we're attached to emotional security and afraid of being rejected, we'll be rejected over and over until we lose that fear. If we're attached to money and afraid of poverty, we will probably have to live with being poor at some point. If we fear cancer or disease (as I did), chances are it will show up in our lives. Only when we know for certain that nothing in this physical world can touch who we truly are, or make us unworthy of divine love, can we see past the attachments to the fears underneath, and sweep them away. Our human suffering is illusory. It will exist only as long as we allow it to define us—as long as we are attached to it.

Michael was attached to physical stuff. He wanted everything—every room, every nook and cranny, every area of life—to feel full and complete. His aversion, his fear, was of emptiness and abandonment. He knew that there was a hole in him that wanted to be filled—but he wasn't ready to identify what was really needed to close that wound. He wasn't ready to align with the divine principle of love, which truly does conquer all.

Reflecting on my life, I can clearly see how each situation, no matter how uncomfortable at the time, paved the way for me to grow into my soul's mission. I can also clearly see how my attachments guided me toward these situations, even though I would never have said at the time that I was seeking those things. Jeremy showed me the lie of beauty and glamour in our modern culture. Tom showed me that attachment to money, success, and power can literally turn your mind inside out. And Michael showed me that even someone born with a silver spoon in his mouth can still choke on it.

This life is a waking dream. It may seem as though we wake up in the morning to the same rooms, the same floors and curtains—but this is because we've anchored ourselves in this aspect of the dream to make it seem more real. If we get rid of our amnesia and remember that our true selves live in the Fourth Dimension, as part of G.O.D., we realize that *we create it all.* We can un-create it, or recreate it, any way we want. When we completely accept that something is true, we make it true; it has to happen. And finally, when all our ideas about what we need to have, and need to do, are dissolved, we come into a place of infinite possibility, where the right path for our soul's growth can become clear, even if it leads in an unexpected direction.

The Good Life isn't all it's cracked up to be; it certainly isn't worth suffering for. The glamour I was so in love with at the start of my career as a sky goddess wasn't what I was really seeking. I realize now that what I really wanted was freedom—and in the pursuit of that freedom, I learned to rely on myself and my connection with G.O.D., which will always point me in the best direction for my soul's continued expansion. True freedom doesn't come from wealth or prestige, but from the certainty of infinite possibility in every day.

And so, when I had finally identified my attachments completely, down to the deepest level of myself, I was lifted out of my marriage to Michael with a minimum of strife. My material things were left behind and I was flying free once more—but this time, I was on my own private jet, and the destination was entirely up to me.

CHAPTER NINE

Skydiving

"If you want to see perfection,

change your perception."

~ Rebecca Tripp

I spent thirty-five years in the sky, and in that time, I never got tired of looking out of the windows of the plane. Each glimpse of the immensity of the Pacific Ocean, or of mountains made tiny by our lofty perspective, helped me remember that there is a larger order at work in everything. In the same way, when we acknowledge ourselves as being one with the Universe, we can look beyond our own transitory suffering to see the big picture.

What we can experience in this moment is not the whole of what's out there. We are, indeed, the children of

G.O.D.; we are babies in utero, waiting to be born into a new way of thinking. Unlike a physical birth, the time and circumstances of our delivery are entirely up to us.

In 2006, after separating from Michael and setting myself up in a lovely garden apartment in Providence, Rhode Island, I came to the full realization of my life's purpose: to assist people to alleviate their suffering through the knowledge and application of metaphysical and spiritual wisdom. I realized that I have the power to create change simply by sharing my story and teaching the techniques I've learned over the course of a lifetime. Everything in my life thus far—every experience, every relationship, every trauma, every triumph—has prepared me to walk this path.

After nearly four decades of traveling, I have truly become a Traveler.

Taking the Leap

Subjective consciousness is made up of imagination and visualization. Both are tools we can utilize to create our world in the way that is most beneficial to our mission here on Earth. We visualize things we have already experienced or seen. We imagine what we want to see—and, as we know, whatever can be imagined can be invented! Neville Goddard, one of the greatest modern teachers of creative visualization, went so far as to say that imagination is God, because its power for creation is limitless.

Taking the leap into this way of thinking is very much akin to jumping out of an airplane. You're in freefall for a while, flailing around, totally unsure of the outcome. There's no up or down, no North or South, and no guarantee that you'll land where you planned. There's no guarantee that your parachute will open, either—but chances are, it will, eventually. Either way, it's pretty much assured that you will emerge from the experience a changed person.

Experienced skydivers know that the only way to achieve control in freefall is to surrender. If you watch them in action, you'll see that their limbs are aligned but not stiff; their movements are slow, deliberate, and minimal. When you launch yourself into a metaphysical journey, the same principles apply. If you try to control every little thing all the time, the results will be chaotic. However, if you visualize your ultimate outcome and allow your experience to unfold in trust, you'll have a much better chance of a smooth landing.

Once you've made the leap into metaphysical thinking, you will be in that state of freefall for as long as it takes for you to learn to surrender and let G.O.D.'s divine energy carry you. Once you're back on solid ground, the world may look different than it did when you left. I know many people (including myself) whose marriages have deteriorated because their spiritual practices no longer allowed them to remain in unhealthy relationships. At the ages of fifty, sixty, or even seventy, they're stepping out into the unknown, changing course, and taking a chance. It's beautiful, actually. The Rules are peeling away from their lives like ancient damask paper from a wall, revealing the blank plaster canvas beneath. The possibilities for what can be painted there are infinite.

I won't lie: it's a lot of work to turn your life around. I was fifty-nine when I separated from Michael, and I felt like a massive cruise ship trying to make a U-turn in a narrow river. There were definitely stuck points—but all I had to do was push a little bit, and a breakthrough would come. With each small shift, my course became clearer.

For almost the entirety of my marriage to Michael, I suffered from Lyme disease. I didn't know at first what was wrong. One day, out of the blue, I woke up with extreme back and neck pain. Over the next few days, it got so bad that I could hardly turn my head.

I went to a traditional Western doctor, and was told that I was dealing with symptoms of menopause. Hormone replacement therapy was recommended, but there was no way I was putting that stuff in my body. Instead, I tried herbal treatments like wild yam and evening primrose oil, but they didn't help. The pain just kept getting worse.

When the pain spread to my hips, I made an appointment with a bone specialist. After a bone density test revealed no abnormalities, the doctor told me to stop wasting his time.

"I can't play basketball anymore either," he said derisively. "You're getting old, just like the rest of us. Deal with it."

So I did—until my hair started falling out. Then, I panicked.

Turns out, Westport, MA is the Lyme disease capital of the world. And yet, none of the doctors in the area were testing for it at that time. Everyone seemed reluctant to give a positive diagnosis, perhaps because the condition was so expensive to treat. It took nearly four years to figure out what was wrong with me—and the diagnosis didn't even come from a doctor.

I happened to mention my symptoms to a friend of mine, a restaurant owner in Westport. Turns out, her entire family had been treated for Lyme at one time or another. She just looked at me and said, "Make them test you."

So I did, and they did. The positive diagnosis sent me into a spiral of fear. All of a sudden, everyone in Westport was talking about this monstrous ailment, and the lives it had destroyed. I resolved to do whatever I needed to do to kick this thing. Antibiotics, immune suppressants, herbs, Ayurvedic treatments, mud wraps, detox diets… You name it, I tried it. The treatments made my pain manageable, but it never went away completely. Despite all my efforts at healing, I was still sick.

Fast forward several years. I was separated, living alone, looking forward to a new life of adventure and magic. My life with Michael was firmly in the past—except for this awful, lingering illness. After doling out my daily dosage of pharmaceuticals and vitamins on this particular morning, I looked down at the pile of pills in my hand. Was this what my hard-won new life was going to look like? Would I really have to swallow mountains of medicine every day for the rest of my life? Was I going to live my life around my illness, constantly navigating the restrictions my "spacesuit" imposed on me?

Not a chance.

It was like a switch flipped in my brain. It didn't matter what The Rules said about the incurability of Lyme disease. "The Rules don't apply to G.O.D.," I reminded myself. "I am a perfect child of the Universe, and perfect health is my birthright!" I taught this truth to students all over the country, and I believed it with my whole heart. I'd been healed before; I'd seen dozens of healings since. So why hadn't I thought to use it on myself? Because Lyme disease was "incurable?" Impossibility had never stopped me before.

I tossed the pills in the trash. Every bottle on my cluttered medicine shelf followed. As I sank into my spiritual consciousness, I felt health and vitality spreading through my body, my cells realigning and regenerating.

After that day, my cruise ship (and my hips) finally came unstuck. There were no more symptoms, not even a twinge. I was able to steer again. My body was back in my control, and it was full steam ahead. The only question was where to go.

Bombs

Our thoughts create our reality. If the three-dimensional realm of our human perception is all we think about, then that is all that will exist to us. G.O.D. is not present *unless we are reflecting G.O.D.*

My spiritual education came to me one puzzle piece at a time over the course of a lifetime—but now I could see the full picture of my reality emerging. It was time for me to go beyond my comfort zone, beyond even the Silva UltraMind method that I was currently teaching. If I was going to continue to fill in my puzzle, I needed to broaden my perspective yet again.

José Silva once said that when we're working on a project that will help mankind, all the spiritual help we need will show up to assist us. Such was the case with me. The assistance I needed showed up quite unexpectedly, in the form of clothes.

Yes, clothes.

In 2009, having returned to Westport once again, I stopped by a favorite boutique to check out the sale rack. I ended up buying two dozen professional-looking outfits. I had no idea why I was buying all of these clothes: I was traveling less, and there were few places for me to wear them in sleepy Westport. But I *had* to have these outfits. I bought so much that I couldn't fit it all in my car: I had to go back the next day to pick up the remainder!

The next night, I spent a few moments in prayer before I went to sleep. "Please show me how I'm going to use all these beautiful new clothes," I asked.

The answer came to me in my dreams, loud and clear: *Go and work part-time at the Christian Science church in Boston.* I recognized the speaker immediately. His was the same deep, male voice that told me I'd be leaving New York after my separation from Jeremy.

3:00 a.m. found me furiously typing keywords into an internet search engine. Lo and behold, a job listing for a part-time tour guide had been posted just a few hours before! I filled out the online application and hit "submit" before I could even process what I was doing. I mean, I'd studied Christian Science, and its principles were at the core of my spiritual healings, but I'd never been a member of the church per se. Was I really ready to make that leap?

The answer, of course, was yes. I was ready to educate a broad group of people from all walks of life, and what better way to do so than as a tour guide?

On Christmas Day, 2009 (the day before I was scheduled to start my new job at the First Church of Christ, Scientist), an attempted terrorist attack on Northwest Airlines Flight 253 was diffused by the passengers and flight crew. Since 9/11, travelers have been a lot more alert when it comes to suspicious activity. This time, their watchfulness averted a potential disaster.

Seeing the news coverage brought me back to the last year of my flying career. It seemed all the self-defense training they'd put us through had come in useful for this new generation of Stews. As odd as it seemed, part of me wished I had been there. What an amazing spiritual learning experience that takedown must have been!

I went to bed that night thinking about bombs.

In my dream, I was alone in a hotel room on an island. The phone on my bedside table rang, and when I picked up, a voice on the other end told me that terrorists were planting atomic bombs all around the world. "Trainees are needed," the voice said. "People who can learn to deactivate these bombs. You have been chosen. Will you take the assignment?"

Even as I slept, I felt a tremendous chill run through me. This task would be difficult and dangerous, but I had to accept. I had been called because I had the right qualifications to be of service to the human race.

"I'll take the job," I told the voice.

Upon waking, I realized that I'd agreed to a monumental task. Those "atomic bombs" being planted represent the worst manifestations of the human condition of separateness: fear, hatred, bigotry, envy, vengeance, greed. These volatile energies need to be deactivated in order for the world to come into a greater balance of peace and harmony, and allow the true presence of G.O.D. to be felt.

To this day, whenever someone I meet in a workshop or in the church has an "Ah-ha!" moment, I visualize a little bomb diffused. As Mary Baker Eddy wrote in her text, *Science and Health with Key to the Scriptures,* "The power of God brings deliverance to the captive. No power can withstand divine love."

The End is the Beginning

During the last year of my flying career, I walked into the flight office at John F. Kennedy International Airport to check in for my flight to California.

"How's it going?" the flight scheduler asked.

"Things are great. I'm working on learning to fly."

He looked up at me quizzically. "What do you mean? You're getting on a plane in twenty minutes."

"I mean, without the airplane. I'm mastering the ability to go anywhere just by thinking about it. You know, teleportation. Astral projection. That kind of thing."

He laughed out loud. "Whatever, sweetheart. Have fun in Fairyland."

I did. Not long after that conversation, I immersed myself in a meditation where I hopped all over the planet. I thought of Costa Rica, and immediately I could smell the rainforest, and feel the moist, hot air on my face. I thought of Tokyo, and I could feel the energy of that city rushing all around me. Everywhere I wanted to be, there I was. It was like the entire planet was contained in my mind, and all I had to do to access any location was to imagine myself there. It was the most incredible experience of my spiritual life to date.

We are everywhere we want to be. If we can imagine it, we can create it. This is the great truth of life: *we are what we think we are.* As we change our thought, we change our reality. The power of creation resides within us.

I could close this book by telling you that I'm living in Shangri La with a coven of ascended masters—but, like Dorothy in the Wizard of Oz, I'm saying, "There's no place like home." My mind has the power to catapult me anywhere I desire to be, and I travel in this way quite often. In body, however, I've chosen to remain here on the ground in Massachusetts, spreading my spiritual message to an ever-growing group of curious Travelers, diffusing bombs, and experiencing an ever-deepening connection to my fourth-dimensional self. My life isn't perfect, but I'm perfectly happy with it. After all, I've created it!

They say that the journey is as important as the destination—but I would venture to say that the journey *is* the destination, and it's more spectacular than we can possibly imagine when we set foot on the path. Along my road, I've found faith, trust, and persistence. I've left a lot of baggage behind, and I know I'll travel even lighter in the future.

Through metaphysics, I've discovered the greatest gift any human being can hope to receive on this three-dimensional plane: true inner peace. Life's classroom still holds many lessons for me, but I already have all the tools I need to pass my tests.

I hope that the experiences I've shared with you in this book help you along your path, Traveler. May the blessings of G.O.D. guide you on your journey, and may the divine principles of love, health, abundance, oneness, and reciprocity always be manifest in your life. You deserve all of these blessings and more, because you are a soul with a body, and you exist.

And above all, remember: *you are not in the airplane, the airplane is in you.*

About the Authors

Rebecca Tripp is a self-proclaimed "metaphysical junkie," and an avid teacher and student of metaphysics, magic, and miracles. Her thirty-five year career as a sky goddess with United Airlines, combined with her love of travel, set the stage for her amazing manifestation of a life lived intentionally. Her life experience and deep sense of spiritual connection have helped hundreds of people discover the power of thought and reclaim the power to create their lives.

Rebecca currently lives in Massachusetts, and leads workshops and retreats nationally and globally. Learn more about her at www.rebeccatripp.com.

Bryna René is an accomplished freelance author, editor, musician, and yoga instructor. She is the editor of the bestselling anthologies, *A Juicy Joyful Life* and *Embracing Your Authentic Self* (2010 and 2011, Inspired Living Publishing), as well as numerous other books on conscious entrepreneurship, metaphysics, and self-awakening. She currently lives in Providence, Rhode Island with her gondolier husband, Marcello, and their venerable Siamese cat.

Learn more about Bryna's work at www.wordsbyaphrodite.com.